"Growing a business on your ow[...] undertaking - there is no one to empathise with you, to reinforce you are 'doing things right' - or wrong! Den's courses are very well put together and based on his real world experience - his camera skills and business advice are excellent. I always look forward to his emails - there is always something insightful and useful in them."
Simon Morton, Aldershot, UK

"I have always respected your hard stance approach to taking the art of filmmaking and making it a business. After our first call you helped instil the confidence and focus I needed to take my business to the next level."
Thaddeus Setla, Benicia, CA

"I have been using Den Lennie as an online coach for a few years now and the tools and techniques I have newly acquired or had reaffirmed have given me the skills and confidence that I needed to just get on with the job without a fuss. Whether you are just starting out or a seasoned professional, there is something in every one of Den's sessions for everyone."
Graham Gall, Canberra, Australia

"Den's video tutorials are always worth the time and money invested, with real-world problem solving, kit and people. They are entertaining and educating in one sitting. You can't get a better bang-for-buck than that :) Thanks Den."
Matt Aindow, Manchester, UK

"Technology is changing our business. We need to grasp quickly what is essential and learn how to maximise it. That's where expert judgement comes to the fore. Den, with you we can cut to the chase and benefit from your years of knowledge. Every time I watch one of your videos, I learn something new. We now put these into practice every day we shoot. If you are not evolving you are falling behind. It's that simple."
Tristan Parry, Sydney, Australia

"I like how Den provides a solid foundation in the basics. Through the three online courses and video tutorial series I've done with F-Stop Academy over the last two years, I've become more confident facing the practical challenges of everyday shooting, including mixed lighting situations, capturing sufficient b-roll in a systematic way, and working with sound. Seeing Den on set on the tutorial videos provides the first-hand examples that I have used as a model to shoot my own projects. In short, Den has given a succinct breakdown of the fundamentals of filmmaking so that I have a structure in which to exercise my creativity."
Jesse Barlow, APO, AE

"Den has been an inspiration for me, and with his clear and no nonsense approach I feel more confident as a result of his teachings."
Benoit Laroche, Montreal, Quebec, Canada

"Den is a no BS instructor. So when you take a seminar, you work, usually with your own gear. So when you walk away you have a set of skills that are still fresh in your head. Not a booklet with 100 pages of notes. But it's afterwards that counts, ask anyone who has gotten to know Den, this is a guy who gives a damn if you make it. And he will do whatever he can to help you succeed. He has corresponded with me and looked in on my work from time to time to encourage or to say, "What the hell is that, mate?" And he shares what he knows willingly."
Stuart Van Dorn, Chicago, Illinois, USA

"Den and the F-Stop Academy is the one stop shop for everything film making. Den's courses are fantastic; he delivers everything in simple concise actionable chunks and at the same time is very entertaining. Thanks Den for helping me get to the next level."
Josh Littlefield, Melbourne, Australia

"Without your guidance and intensive courses, I would not have been able to shoot my first short film. After days of scouring the web for a crash course in filmmaking, I landed on your site and knew I had found a real gem of information and knowledge that can only come through years and years of experience. Thanks Den for all your support and help."
Jesse Osmer, Arlesheim, Switzerland

"When I started my internet marketing company in 2010, I made a great decision to turn to Den Lennie for some training. He provided information that reduced my learning curve in developing my video production skills, which contributed to my bottom line very quickly. Den knows the business and I really enjoy his teaching style."
Ken Poindexter, Charlotte, NC, USA

"It doesn't get any better than Den! Thoughtful, passionate, caring and very skilful - Mr. Den Lennie is a master at what he does and teaches in a 'no nonsense' and approachable manner that will leave you inspired. I can't recommend him enough!"
Rich Prince, Studio City, California USA

"It has been a pleasure to be a part of the F-Stop Academy learning experience, from workshops to online training materials. I have continually applied what I have learned and it has delivered great results for me. This training has definitely given me a competitive advantage in my film business. Thanks for your support and encouragement."
Clint Regehr, Frisco, TX, USA

"I was struggling to apply the skills I had learned as a filmmaker on 16mm many years ago to the art of digital video. Den and F-Stop Academy have consistently helped me to understand the latest techniques to the point where they are becoming, as before, second nature. I now have the confidence to tackle any assignment, knowing that the F-Stop Academy is right behind me and only a quick email away. Thanks, Den!"
Paul Langley, Sydney, Australia

"Working alone, I appreciate the straight talking style on what is absolutely necessary to succeed in terms of work ethics and attitude. Your emphasis on using elbow grease and solid skills over 'new gear' is exactly what we need to hear in a world where new gear and innovation is constantly shoved in our faces. I thank you most for that!"
Andrew Jones, Tokyo, Japan

"What makes the difference between going to set up a video shoot feeling excited or nervous? It's knowing your tools and how to use them. Everything you do in life is a learned skill. The more you know the more confident you become. Gaining the knowledge I have is to a large part my investment in F-stop academy. The rest is practice, practice and pushing yourself a little bit more each time. Before I met Den I did not foresee me being able to go self-employed doing something that I love. I am now doing that and have the freedom to work when and where I want to. That's a huge difference from having to get up each morning and face the mad commute into London."
Mark Gibson, Oxted, Surrey UK

"The approach is very personally directed, as if Den is talking to me alone. So much so that I feel I have known him for a while. Sort of weird, but that degree of resonance makes me feel we're already great friends. Now, add on top of that, the no-nonsense advice, context, judgment, wisdom and experience that Den offers and it makes for a valuable experience in practical application of these helpful training exercises."
Tom Kalajian, Orange County, CA

"Clear, straight forward information, no bullshit...just what you need to know... Get on it ...NOW!!!"
Brett Moulton, Melbourne, Australia

BUSINESS for FILMMAKERS

Den Lennie

Business For Filmmakers

Copyright 2014 © Den Lennie

www.fstopacademy.com

ISBN 978-1-907308-50-5

First published in Great Britain by Compass Publishing 2014

A catalogue record of this book is available from the British Library

Set and designed by The Book Refinery Ltd

Den Lennie asserts the rights to be identified as the author of this work.

Dedication

Thank you to my lovely wife Sam, who has believed in me and supported me through thick and thin since we started F-Stop Academy in 2009.

To my Mum and Dad for always allowing me to be me and for encouraging me to pursue my dream of becoming a cameraman.

I'd also like to thank Jim Galbreath, Ian Cowie and Paul Gavin without whom my first steps in this industry would have been much harder.

To my friends and colleagues Jon McCulloch and Kat Smith for never allowing me to give up.

To John Brennan and Cal Barton for teaching me how to run a business ethically and with integrity.

And to my dear friend and mentor Darragh Sinnot for being my entrepreneurial coach and inspiration.

And last but by no means least, Dudley our black Pug, who kept me company throughout the writing of the book, and reminds me daily how important it is to enjoy life and have fun.

Contents

Contents

Preface

Congratulations! You have taken a very important step in making your video business a commercial success and ultimately creating a more financially secure future for you and your family.

Now, not everyone is going to like this book, nor are they going to want to believe that what I am about to share with you, is not only true, but works.

I know this because everything in between the covers of this book has been personally tried and tested by me in my own business. This is not theory but real life, fought in the trenches and it includes principles and strategies that will help grow your business so you can be more successful, earn more money and choose the clients you deal with. *I call it freedom.*

But before we begin, a word of warning...

This will not just happen on its own. Neither will reading this book make you successful (although it will get you there faster if you apply everything I am about to share with you). You will need to put effort in, a lot of effort. But if you are going to set up a business then it makes sense that you should give it all you've got because if you are prepared to do now, what most of your friends can't be bothered to, then in five to10 years you can be living a life and have a lifestyle that they cannot ever imagine, because they will either be stuck in their dead end jobs, or a wage slave to the man.

It's very easy to say you are going to start a video production business. Many present the (false) facade that they are a big deal. Do not be fooled into ever believing that the front of house people paraded on social media are (a) real or (b) anything close to what the back of house looks like in a thriving business. I have seen hundreds of people paraded on social media saying, *"really proud to show off our latest reel"*, *"Please, please, Pictures, here's our latest music video (or self-indulgent project)* and, *"…oh, and we're available to shoot your next project."* Then there is *"plonker productions, just in the next new shiny piece of gear, now available for use on your next video."*

Here's the harsh reality… clients for the most part do not give a damn what camera you are using. The only people who are likely to pay any attention are your 'social media friends'.

Let me tell you, of all the serious video production companies and filmmakers I know who are making good money, shooting real commercial projects regularly… they are too damned busy working to spend all day posting updates on Facebook or Twitter. That, my friend, is a harsh fact.

Now *we will* cover advertising in this book in a later chapter but be prepared for a shock when it comes to social media and its effectiveness in generating new business.

My promise to you:

If you want to make more money, get paid what you are worth and have clients love what you do and keep coming back for more then read on because I am going to share with you the exact steps you need to take to make this a reality.

But before we begin, you need to understand something. Most of what you read online and on social media is crap. It's largely full of insecure, ego driven people giving advice on subjects they know little about or are not qualified to advise on. This is especially true when it comes to business advice.

One of my mentors (who retired with a multi million cash fortune at 41) told me, *"never accept business advice from anyone less successful than you"*. This is a vital piece of advice that I want you to nail to the inside of your eyelids. He's been a mentor to me for the last four years and has become a close friend in the process.

One of the things you must get to grips with early on is that your friends, family and other people close to you are most likely not qualified to give you business advice. Yet that will not stop them offering their opinion. Be very wary of opinions - they're like arseholes… everybody has one.

I'm going to repeat this again, *"ONLY EVER TAKE BUSINESS ADVICE FROM SOMEONE WHO IS MORE SUCCESSFUL IN RUNNING A BUSINESS THAN YOU ARE."*

And on that note, a few considerations before you continue:

- ✓ This book is going to tell you it straight.

- ✓ There will be a distinct lack of BS and fluff.

- ✓ I practice what I preach - no theory just facts.

- ✓ Not everything in business, sales and marketing works - don't think - test.

- ✓ JFDI (Just Fucking Do It).

Let's go build your business!

Introduction

Why do you want to run a video production business?

This is not a question I want you to skim over lightly. Often in life you end up falling into jobs, careers and opportunities. One thing leads to another and suddenly you are an accountant...

OK maybe a little extreme, but I do want you to consider what it is exactly you want to do and why? If now is the time for you to create a video business, then strap in, because you're in for one hell of a ride.

The democratisation of affordable video has undoubtedly created a new wave of filmmakers and opportunities. But do not be mistaken in thinking that buying all the gear and setting up a website is enough to generate adequate revenue to pay for all of the costs of running a business and generating new leads as well as having some profit to live off and enjoy.

Thankfully, you're already in safe hands because in the next 200 or so pages, I'm going to give you a solid marketing and business blueprint - that if you implement - will not only help you create a solid business but will go way beyond and generate a sustainable income affording you freedom and fun.

Who this book is for:

This book is primarily aimed at helping existing video production businesses that already generate its main income from video production and want to break away from low priced jobs and earn a decent living.

It's designed to help those filmmakers who feel like perhaps they aren't charging enough for their services and feel trapped in a spiralling price driven market.

If you are just starting out or are currently employed full time, then this book will give you all the tools needed to make an informed decision about setting up and running a video production business. Armed with this new 'battle tested' information and resource you can then decide if it is indeed the right path for you.

How to get the best from this book:

While each chapter is a standalone section in this book, I strongly recommend that you read it chronologically. It will make much more sense to you if you do this, and, as I reveal each marketing principle and business building resource, you will begin to form your own ideas on how to create similar systems for your own enterprise. Take notes, highlight pages and re-read the book as you need to.

Creating a successful video production business relies on automated marketing systems that bring in an endless stream of pre qualified 'ideal clients'. If you read my story that I share with you at the end of this book, then you'll know what I've had to face to get where I am now. You will also learn how much emphasis I put on 'relationship selling'. It's often labelled as consultative selling in traditional business books, but in essence it's helping people solve their problems before they have even thought of them.

And that is really the common theme throughout this book, solving people's problems and taking away pain because that is how we are wired as human beings. So if you're offering video production services to clients, identifying the pain and taking that away will be fundamental in your success.

If you currently provide a commodity-based service then you are likely to be operating in a price only based market and the last thing you want to be doing is competing on the 'cheapest price' race to the bottom.

Finally, everything in this book I have personally tried, tested and implemented. There is no bullshit in this book. If you follow my advice, implement it and ignore criticism, you will thrive.

If, after doing all of that, you are not making more money and working with better clients as a result, just let me know and I'll send you a full refund for the book and you don't even have to send me it back.

That is my promise to you.

Chapter 1

POSITIONING YOUR BUSINESS

What Does Your Perfect Business Look Like?

It's always a good idea to try and visualise what your ideal business looks like. Given you are about to (or are already) be spending a large proportion of your waking hours for the next five to 10 years working on or thinking about your business, then you may as well make sure you know where you are going with it.

Now everyone is different, but I find that writing down goals and aspirations helps me to retain focus on the final destination. Here are my six top steps to position your business correctly.

Step 1- Pick a niche

One of the most common mistakes I see filmmakers make is that they try too hard to be a 'jack of all trades'. They'll advertise themselves as corporate video production, event filmmakers, PR filmmakers, commercials, weddings, in some cases, and a whole host of other services...(web design, video duplication ... and so on).

Stop!

Generalisation is a *big mistake*, actually, make that a **huge mistake.**

When you dilute your product or service, you commodotise yourself and are opening yourself up to price based buyers. (More on pricing in a later chapter.) You do not want to compete on price.

It's far better to specialise and become the number one choice for your customers in that field. This can be very counterintuitive and will feel uncomfortable for some of you. But remember if this was easy, then everyone would be doing it.

You want to be working towards becoming a specialist. When you are a specialist, and, more importantly, the very best in your field, pricing becomes elastic. If you had a busted leg, you'd want a specialist orthopaedic surgeon working on you right? Not a GP. Think about that for a moment.

Now, I'm not saying you need to be the very best in your country, just perceived as the best to your chosen customer niche, or in your local area - say within a 100 mile radius of where you live and work.

When clients are looking for a video production company, it's highly likely that they are not looking for anything other than someone to come and deliver a result. They certainly don't care what camera you are using and most likely haven't got a clue about sliders, colour grading or any of the other paraphernalia that surrounds video technology. It's all about them feeling comfortable that you are going to be trustworthy enough and skilled enough to deliver the result they want. They are not looking for you to win your next award off the back of their video production.

For the most part, the majority of corporate clients are conservative and want a safe, good looking video that looks as if it could be shown on TV and no one would know the difference.

Step 2 - How to choose your niche

Start by thinking about what you love to shoot. What are your favourite types of client projects? What wouldyou do every day if you could? Once you have figured that out you need to ignore everything else and just focus on building a business around that specialism.

In my corporate production work, I specialise in making launch films for the film and TV manufacturing industry. I love making them; we are very, very good at it, nobody can make them as fast as we can, and as a result of having no competition, we can charge a premium rate for the work. We make good margin on every project, which means we don't have to take very many. That in turn means that my clients get very personal attention from us and they keep coming back for more. It's a win-win situation. They are happy to pay our prices because we over deliver, and they get the results they desire and much more. The bottom line is they see a great deal of perceived value in what we offer to them.

My motto in our production business is: *'Telling Stories That Sell'*.

We give our clients so much more than a video; they get a consultative relationship that extends way beyond just delivering a film.

We make ourselves invaluable to our clients and we make their life easier and so they keep coming back, because it's easy.

By the end of this book, you will have a deep understanding of how to attract clients that come back again and again because you make it easy for them to do business with you.

So think about what your ideal business looks like.

Once you identify that you can begin working on the mechanics that surround it.

Step 3 - Decide how much money you want to make

Money is a topic that not everyone is comfortable discussing. I've never really understood why it is such a taboo subject. Certainly in the UK, where I grew up, talking about money was always, and still is, a big social taboo. Probably something to do with the uptight nature of being British...

It's also interesting to observe how infrequently it is ever talked about online in the filmmaking community. My theory is that most of the active social media commentators are not actually making all that much money. It's easy to parade around talking about how awesome you are and getting snapped with various celebs while filming a job... but when you bump into these same people at trade shows they're often sleeping on a friend's floor and getting the bus to the exhibition, not quite the five star hotels and limos that their Instagram account might display.

Let me be clear. If you want to get a ton of Twitter followers and Facebook fans to validate yourself go and knock yourself out. I don't really give a crap about that - because it really doesn't generate enough direct business to justify the effort. The only way people really vote is with their wallets.

So if you want to make money - then you are gonna have to start cutting that umbilical to social media. Social media will suck your time dry and deliver very few results.

It's a commonly held position by the creative community at large that in order to be creative you can't be seen to be profiting financially.

What a load of old bollocks.

There is absolutely no reason why you should not make a very good living producing corporate films.

It's completely achievable to be generating revenues in excess of $100,000 per year making corporate films. And in many cases, significantly more.

Another good exercise is to create a financial goal sheet.

On this sheet, write down the ideal car you'd like to drive, the ideal house (and location) you'd like to own. Where you'd like to have your business, what type of vacations you'd like to go on and where. How many vacations would you like a year? Perhaps you want to provide for your children's education or future? Maybe you'd like to own a luxury watch? Whatever it is, write it down.

What kind of camera gear and edit equipment would you love to own and use every day if money was no object? Write down what all of that would cost, then you'll have a figure.

Divide what all of that would cost into 12 months and you'll have a sum that you need to achieve every month in order to make it all a reality.

Granted, there are some other factors to consider. Tax, re-investment in equipment and facilities, rent, rates, and other business costs, but the purpose of this exercise is to get you thinking about money and what you really need to have the lifestyle you desire.

So the figure you need to earn to have the lifestyle you want is your starting point. That figure is what you need to be generating after all of your expenses are taken care of and after tax is paid.

It's called your *net profit*.

Now turnover and profit are two very different numbers and high turnover does not automatically mean high profit.

There's an expression I like to use;

'Turnover is for show, profit is for dough.'

Some business owners like to puff their chests out and talk about how much money they make (they are talking about turnover) and how many staff they have, and yet they make marginal profits.

In the new video economy my view is very different. Keep your costs down, don't rent a fancy office in a downtown location and keep your staffing to an absolute minimum. Maintaining manageable overheads will save you a great deal of stress and cash!

Running a business is tough and you have to get tough on yourself and your own spending. It's so easy to start a business and spend money on all sorts of 'business stuff'. You can easily spend $500 on stationary supplies, business cards, headed paper, etc... you don't need any of that. You can create a letterhead on Apple Pages or Microsoft Word and print it out. Also, when you start a business you'll begin getting calls from all sorts of suppliers trying to sell you business services. Especially watch out for the bank that will invite you in for a meeting to discuss insuring your business against all sorts of stuff you simply don't need.

The only insurance you need is public liability for when you're out shooting in public (which means anywhere that is not your office) and employers' liability if you subcontract any roles on a shoot.

That is certainly the case in the UK. I cannot comment on the laws in your country, but you should only insure yourself with the essentials in the beginning. The caveat to that is if you are a freelancer then get some income protection insurance from a specialist media broker.

There are some resources over at www.businessforfilmmakers.com/resources

It's cash that keeps your business from going bust, nothing else. Cash is King. When you have positive cash flow you have options. More businesses go broke through lack of good cash flow than anything else. Protect your cash as much as you can. We'll talk about the importance of cash flow in a later chapter on financials.

Avoid having full time staff until you are generating revenues that make working with freelancers or outsourced help impossible.

I know businesses generating in excess of $500,000 per year with no full time members of staff. You can outsource many, many tasks to freelance specialists. Hiring staff can be the biggest pain you have ever experienced. Avoid it at all costs until such a time when you cannot run your business any other way. You can more than likely be generating significant revenues for many years and not need any full time staff.

Step 4 - Identify who your ideal client is and why

Defining who you ideally want to be doing business with is a *very important step* in developing your business.

Take the car industry for example: Do you think Audi are looking to attract Ford Focus owners? Probably not. More likely, they want to attract BMW or Mercedes owners. They are looking for a certain type of customer, with a certain ability to pay for a luxury car. The type of customer who appreciates quality and is in the fortunate position of not having to buy the cheapest vehicle.

Taking air travel as another example, in the last 12 months, I've taken eight long haul return flights, with a total of 16 individual sectors. Each time in business class. I also got upgraded to first class on one BA flight.

The airline industry has three levels of service; economy, business and first class. I can tell you that after flying in business class, I don't ever want to fly economy ever again. And as you'd expect, the experience of flying in business and first class is wildly different than in economy.

Yet all the passengers are sitting inside the same aircraft and all arrive at the same destination at exactly the same time.

Business class fares are typically three to four times the price of a standard economy ticket and first class can be as much as 12 times the price of an economy seat.

What blows me away every time I fly business class?

It's just how busy it always is. Often, it's full or nearly full. It goes to show that there are lots of customers prepared to pay three to four times the standard rate in exchange for increased levels of service, comfort and perceived value. And that value only has to be perceived in its simplest form. Yes you have to deliver a higher standard of luxury, comfort and service to a business class passenger, but for the airline it does not necessarily cost them three to four times as much to fulfil that service.

By charging more they need less passengers to make the same revenue, and therefore can deliver a more personal service to those customers. Business class passengers are way more profitable for an airline than economy passengers.

Now translate that analogy to your video production business. Who would you rather be doing business with? Do you want four x the economy passengers coming through your doors or does a smaller number of the business class passengers paying four times as much, sound more appealing?

If you specialise, focus on serving your chosen niche and offer a superior service, then you can choose the business class route and you'll not only reach your desired revenue targets, but you'll also end up dealing with a better class of customer. You'll have fewer headaches and be much more fulfilled on a daily basis.

Not all customers were created equally and it is a myth that all should be treated the same. Like in our airline analogy, you would expect the service levels given to first class passengers to be somewhat more personalised and exclusive than the ones given to passengers travelling in economy. And rightly so if they are paying 12x as much for their ticket. That is how commerce works. If you want to make money, get to grips with it. There are too many entitled 'poor me' filmmakers around, *"Oh, but I'm a struggling artist,"* yeah, really? Then get off your arse, stop complaining and do something about it. You are ultimately responsible for your own success in life, no one else is.

Choose your customers carefully, and don't be misled into thinking you don't have a choice because you absolutely do. It's your business and you decide who you let in. Simple. Running a business is not a democracy. Your business - your rules!

Step 5 - Create a customer avatar

An avatar is your perfect customer - described in detail.

This exercise is very important in attracting your ideal customer. You need to write this one down.

Think of this as customer profiling. If you are already in business then you will have a client (hopefully) that you really like dealing with. They are fair and communicate clearly what their ultimate objective is. They understand that you have costs, they realise that you are in business to make profit and value what you do so pay you what you are worth and are happy to do so because of the value they receive in return. They only work Monday to Friday and respect your weekends... And they always come back to you for more because they trust you.

If that is not your customer then let's help you find one just like that.

Here are some questions to answer about your ideal customer avatar:

- Are they male or female?
- What is their name?
- How old are they?
- How long have they been in their current role?
- What is their relationship status?
- What is their job title?
- How long have they been doing that job?
- How much of that role involves commissioning video?
- Who else do they influence?
- Do they have a team?
- What kind of car do they drive?
- What kind of house do they live in?
- Do they own or rent their house?

- What do they do in their spare time?
- How much do they earn annually?
- Do they have kids? If so, how many? How old? Boys or girls?
- How do they spend their time away from work?
- What kind of vacation do they like to go on?
- What kind of music do they listen to?
- Are they into sports? If so what sports
- Do they like the arts?

This list can go on and on. The deeper you dig into how your ideal customer looks, the easier it will be to attract more customers like them.

This avatar should then be written up on a one page A4 letter and printed out. Give your avatar a name and every time you create any marketing communication, write to that avatar. By writing to one person, your emails and other marketing communications will resonate with your target customer.

Why? Because it's human nature to be attracted to more people like us. It's actually very simple psychology. We are pack animals in our nature and we naturally migrate to 'people like us', and so when you begin communicating with a target market you are purposefully sending messages out that only a certain type of person will respond to.

Now, there is a downside to this type of marketing. You will upset people. When you look to attract a certain type of person you will repel others, but this is a good thing. Remember, you only want to attract your ideal customer. Many will come into contact with you and try to tell you how you should be running your marketing. Ignore them. It's your business and you are only looking for a certain type of customer.

You do need to grow a thick skin. When you set your stake in the sand, you will attract people and also get on the nerves of people who you don't want as customers. But that will not stop them trying to tell you how wrong you are and that you should be doing more of X and less of Y. That is the price of success and honestly you will hit a few idiots along the way. You just need to maintain focus on why you are doing it and ignore them.

Step 6 - How to market to your ideal client

Now that you have clearly identified the ideal customer you wish to attract, you now need to find them and begin building a relationship with them.

This is actually much easier than you might at first think. This is because if you have created your avatar correctly, and you know what kind of revenues you need to build the business and lifestyle you desire, all you need to do now if find the right customers to help you fund it.

Targeting your ideal customer

So, if you look at the avatar you created, this is a pretty comprehensive profile of how this person lives his or her life. Next thing to do is get an insight into what publications they read, what websites they visit and what social media channels they are on. Facebook, LinkedIn and Google/YouTube are good starting points.

The truth is, it is entirely dependent on who you are looking to attract and what level of production spend they are likely to invest with you. It's more likely that a senior corporate manager will be on LinkedIn and less likely that they will be on Facebook... but you never know so you have to test to discover where your ideal customer is hiding.

In truth, most relationships are formed over many months and years and it is unlikely you will be handed a $65,000 budget in your first year. But if you do no marketing then you can safely assume your business will never grow to the size you desire and achieve the revenues you pursue.

I'll be talking a lot about marketing in this book.

That's because it is *vital* to the success of your video production business. I've seen too many filmmakers think that buying a load of gear and having a website is all you have to do. Well, you are reading this book so I know you are much smarter than the average filmmaker.

The purpose of marketing is to make sure that when your ideal target client needs the service you offer, then he or she will pick up the phone and think of you and noone else.

You achieve this by building a relationship through *continual engagement with that prospect.*

If you are on my email list then you will have been through that process with me. At some point you will have either (a) bought a product from us or, more likely, (b) signed up for a free video series or free report first.

I then sent you somewhere in the region of 26 emails that offered valuable free guidance and advice. This was no accident and was specifically to build a relationship with you. By offering you a free report, I'm starting our relationship by giving to you. I then offer you an opportunity to get to know me and this gives you a chance to decide if you trust what I was telling you, if you like what I am telling you and therefore if I might be someone who you'll trust to help you evolve as a filmmaker.

Not everyone who signs up becomes a customer, but that's OK because I don't want everyone who signs up. It's a two way street. Like I've been telling you, you are only looking for a specific kind of customer.

You absolutely do not want to subscribe to the commonly held opinion that all prospects should be treated equally. I'll give you an example. I recently had a guy contact our helpdesk and ask a question about a course. Now I was busy running our first *'How To Shoot Sequences'* intake and like I say, I give more attention to my fee paying clients than my not yet customers... Anyway, I did not reply to this guy's question straight away and so six days later he sent me a shitty email...

We'll call him John - here's what he wrote verbatim:

"It's now five days since I requested this information. If you're looking to sell your courses, failing to answer this sort of inquiry is not a good look. Frankly, I am disappointed in your lack of response, and thus I start to wonder if your promises of quality training also lack integrity. You are certainly not the cheapest, but I have had better response from other sites that do not charge as much as you do. I will wait another few days before taking my business elsewhere. Perhaps this might stir your response along."

Now, what this guy failed to understand is that whether or not he buys a course or not makes very little difference to me...

Now, it turns out he had not yet received the 26 emails and happened to stumble on our site while looking for training. (Unqualified lead.)

I've since changed this because I actually don't want people to stumble across our site. Now what happens is that in order to access our website at *www.fstopacademy.com* you only have one option, you sign up for our email list or you don't get in....

Counterproductive you say?

Not at all, see I only want a certain type of customer and it's my business, my rules.

This way I get to control our relationship, only sending out bits of content at one time. I am then able to get a better understanding of who the prospect is, what they are looking to achieve and what their goals, aspirations and expectations are. Then we can make a decision about whether that person is a good fit for what we offer and what the most appropriate path is for them going forwards.

And likewise they can decide if what we offer is right for them. This is consultative selling, and for the most part its automated.

I'll explain how we achieve this in later chapters, but what it means is that my prospects are taken on an automated journey until such times as they buy something, then they get my attention.

This leaves me free to focus on my paying customers and clients - which is exactly as it should be.

So back to John. Here is how I replied:

Hi John

Den here.

Please accept my apologies that this ticket has been missed. I have to take responsibility for this. We have recently launched a new online program that has consumed us and I have just spent three weeks in Asia helping Sony launch their A7s camera. We missed the ticket - I am sorry.

It sounds like you have found some alternative classes that seem to suit your budget better.

If you cannot afford our training at this level then it's unlikely we'll be a good fit for your needs going forwards as the classes you are looking at are at the entry level for our pricing - they only get more expensive from here.

However, the price and perceived expense is entirely subjective, especially when relating how much the average filmmaker spends on camera gear. Also, if a $147 investment to tap into my brain and get insights gleaned from 20 or so years lighting on location seems expensive to you, then we are almost certainly not a good fit for each other.

What's more, I can safely assume that you've been trying to get the lighting right on your own videos without success and I can also safely assume you've spent some time searching on YouTube and the internet for a solution... I'm guessing you have spent many hours looking at the options...

But you want to tell me that my classes are more expensive than 'others' out there. Good! I'm glad, because my classes offer far more value than anything else out there... in fact, I don't have any competition.

I have thousands of students all over the world and in Australia who have benefited from my training and continue to come back for more and more.

In answer to your question, "So my question is, are your courses going to give me the sort of information and training that I will need to get the best out of my style of cameras?"

If you think it's the camera that makes a difference then we almost certainly will not get on.

There are many hours of free resources on our website and you have downloaded the free three reports. If you've read them then you will have a good solid understanding of what steps contribute to making a video - and it goes way beyond the camera.

It seems to me that you want guarantees that if you buy my program all your problems will be solved.

This is why it makes me nervous to take you on as a customer...

Normally I'd be saying no thank you at this stage - but I'm willing to give you the benefit of the doubt.

My advice is to go and study the free lighting resources on our website.

http://www.fstopacademy.com/category/learn/lighting-tips/

If after watching these it is not clear how we teach and what value we offer then I politely suggest you go and buy your training from the other sources you talk of.

And finally... I do not care for threats...

"I will wait another few days before taking my business elsewhere. Perhaps this might stir your response along."

If we do not have what you are looking for then please please do take your business elsewhere - it would make no sense for you to buy something that is not right for you, and I don't need any customers who are not entirely comfortable buying our resources.

Every success in your endeavour.

Warmly.

Den.

How much are you worth? How much is your time worth? The last thing you want or need in your life is people who are yet to buy anything giving you shit about how you should run your business. When people do this to me they always get a stern response.

The outcome? Well after a somewhat apologetic email in response from John, he bought a program. Now we'll see how he gets on and with any luck our rocky start will only strengthen in time.

My business my rules.

Notice also how I did not flinch under his *"I've seen cheaper stuff elsewhere"* that was him flexing his *"I'll choose how I spend my money and you better be nice to me or I'll spend it elsewhere..."* and how did I reply: *"... go on, be my guest, because I only want customers who are the best fit for me and my business."*

The last thing I want is anyone to invest with us if the solution is not right for them, but more importantly, I do not want to deal with someone who is not a great fit for me and my business.

And neither should you!

> *You want to repel the price buyers and attract only your ideal customers.*

Chapter 2
CREATING A PLAN FOR YOUR BUSINESS

Show Me The Money

Let's not beat about the bush here. If you have set up a business then the number one priority should be *to make money*.

If you are not seriously focused on profit, then you need to take a long hard look at yourself and ask why did you decide to set up a business? If you only want to shoot for art or fun then you are an amateur – it's that simple.

Being an amateur is OK - but this book is about business, and to run a successful business you have to make a profit.

All too often I hear pathetic excuses about 'art' and 'selling out' from people who simply do not have the balls to make it in business. Business is hard and it's unforgiving. If you want adulation, then get yourself a Twitter account, give everything you do away for free and answer every daft question that gets thrown at you… people will love you publicly and maybe you can feel good about 'sharing so much'.

Similarly, if you ever do a job for free, in the vain hope that later on a client will come back to you and pay you, then you are deluded.

Fashion brands are notorious for this sneaky tactic.

They'll call you up, wave their brand under your nose, talk up how much work they have and how much video they'll be needing going forwards. This could grow into a great opportunity for you in the future... but, (there's always a but) we don't have much (or any) budget for this project, so if you could do this one for free, we can get to see your work and then we'll pay you for the next project.

The trouble with that is, you won't make any money and after giving one job away for free, when you *do start* to charge your clients will be shocked: *"but you used to give us that for free!"*

People who do free are not valued... period.

Clients will often use this tactic to get a discount from you. *"If you could do us a deal on the pilot, then when the series comes in you'll get first shout and we'll have a proper budget."* If this happens to you, run!

In all my years of doing broadcast TV, the pilot budget never went up when the programme was commissioned. Their attitude was always, *"you did the pilot for x and so there's no more money for the series."* (Usually followed by – *"can we have a better deal because it's a series?"*)

The same thing happens with corporate clients. There is very often a lure of more work. It almost always never comes to anything.

Work for agreed sums, and if someone is after a deal, there are ways to show *value add* or *perceived discounts*, but only if they are willing to concede something in return.

For example, if a client wants a price break, then I may agree to a percentage saving if they pay the invoice in full, up front. But this is a very rare occurrence and I usually save it as a negotiation tool.

Large corporations have very strict payment terms in place and while the person you may be dealing with is looking to bring a line itemised budget in at a certain cost (to satisfy his or her departmental spend), the accounts department almost always run things very strictly, with very little room to bend.

So, when a marketing department wants a deal, they have to go and speak to accounts and see if they can make an exception so that you can get paid faster. I find this approach is a good relationship tester, because if your contact really wants to save some money and you can get paid quickly, then that's a fair deal for both parties. If they cannot get you paid faster, the quote remains unchanged.

I once waited 96 days to be paid *over £76,000*, purely because of corporate administration and bureaucracy. Now, given that there were a lot of hard production costs to cover, I was significantly out of pocket. Normally I insist on 50% up front, but in this case it was a trusted client with whom I had a 10 year + relationship. Still, it pushed our relationship a little too close to the edge for my liking.

The next time I did work for that client, they wanted to bring a budget in *£6,000 under what had been quoted*. We cut some shoot days and reduced some post production time, but in order to make it workable, I said we could do it if we were paid in 45 days.

At first they said it couldn't be done, so I said, *"ok, no deal."* Then, after a few days, they figured out a way to have me paid by another supplier they used, who was already set up with a 30 day payment contract. It took a bit of persuasion, but the net result was that I got paid in 45 days and not 90.

> *You must create an incentive if any kind of deal is to be done,*
> *otherwise you are just knocking money off for no reason.*

Cash is King in any business. Forget profit and loss for a moment - **cash flow is what keeps you afloat**. Nothing else.

The most important number in your business is how much you have in the bank. With cash you have options.

You can have the greatest *potential profit* on a job, but if you don't get paid or have to wait months, it could send you under.

Never ever over stretch yourself more than you can afford to lose.

Large corporations (certainly in Europe) make it policy not to pay suppliers until they have to, and if you start to do work for larger corporations it's likely they will insist on a contract of services agreement prior to commencement on any project. This will generally be a non-disclosure agreement and will likely set out their payment terms. 60, 90 or 120 days are not uncommon and only kick in once the invoice has been received and has the correct purchase order reference completed in the way they like. If not, you risk it being rejected.

Cash Flow Planning

Cash is King, Cash is King, Cash is King!

Positive cash flow is everything. In business, it is your **single most important number** by a mile.

You should know how much *working capital* you have at the bank on any given week. *Working capital* is cash that is yours to use as you wish. So once all of your liabilities have been paid, money set aside for taxes, and any other fixed monthly outgoings have been accounted for, the amount that is left is your *working capital.*

Regular running costs in your business can soon mount up. It's important to have a spreadsheet with each item, the monthly costs and the date when that bill is due. This is known as a *liability.* *Liabilities* are all of your monthly outgoings.

Click here for an example of a cash flow spreadsheet www.businessforfilmmakers.com/cashflowtemplate

I'm pretty certain you know what it feels like to have no cash - I certainly remember what that feels like. You feel hopeless, alone and unable to do anything without stressing about the lack of cash in your pocket.

It's also interesting how isolated you can feel when you are broke.

No cash means problems, and lots of them. Lack of cash leads to desperation. So, when you do get a call for a job, you are so desperate for the money you say yes to anything and at any price.

This is a terrible position to be in - in any negotiation. When you are on the back foot financially, you will not have the luxury to walk away from a deal that is not in your favour.

Making sales, factoring in profit margin and managing day-to-day costs is all important, but you must have a spreadsheet that details your monthly cash flow movements and you need to be on top of that figure on a daily and weekly basis.

Plenty of businesses look profitable on paper, but still go under due to bad cash flow management.

Getting paid by clients will potentially be one of your biggest headaches. There is no worse feeling than completing a project that you have slaved over and are very happy with, and hopefully the client is also very happy with, only to then wait months to be paid. It can really spoil a relationship, let alone cause you endless sleepless nights and anxiety as you try to maintain a business.

5 Tips for better cash flow

1. Make sure that you are the only one with access to the bank account. As the business owner you should sign every cheque and authorise every single payment that comes and goes in and out of your business bank account.

2. By signing off every payment you become intimately entwined in the daily costs of running your business. You can then assess if what you're spending money on is an essential part of your business. If not, then cancel it and stop paying for it.

3. You are legally responsible for filing taxes and VAT (or GST in some countries). I've heard of many creatives who charge the additional taxes only to receive all the money and forget

to set aside the 10% to 20% of VAT (or GST). They then spend it naively thinking that the cash is all 'working capital'. Worse still they don't set aside 20 to 30% for taxation liabilities due at the end of the financial year. So be wise, and as soon as you receive an invoice, take the VAT or GST, set it aside in a savings account and then ignore it. That way, when your quarterly bill comes in, you have the money there ready to pay - this greatly reduces stress. Not to mention keeping you out of jail for non-payment.

4. Create a cash flow forecast spreadsheet. This is a simple document that I use to list invoices that have been sent and expected payment dates. That way you can forecast when cash is expected in and it allows you to be ready to chase your client if payment does not hit when expected.

5. Review your monthly liabilities regularly. It may be that you signed up for a recurring payment early in your business start-up that is no longer required. Constantly review your outgoings and cancel services you're no longer using. There is no need to be paying for stuff you're not using every day. Your business needs will constantly change.

Learn to say 'no' to price based buyers

The majority is almost always wrong

Which is why I am never surprised when I come across discussions about rates and what 'clients are willing to pay'. Firstly, 'what clients are willing to pay' is subjective and dependent on a number of factors. None of which any of us can fully be aware of, let alone make sweeping statements about.

Social media is rife with this kind of nonsense. It seems to attract big mouthed 'self-proclaimed experts'. Another place for such discussion is professional video organisations or 'institutes'.

Please be very wary of whom you listen to when it comes to this topic.

> *Only ever take financial advice from someone who is more successful than you. Period!*

Some of these organisations with discussion forums are nothing more than a platform for 'has beens' and 'past its' to kick tyres around, bitching about how it used to be in the good old days.

Sadly these discussion groups are often dominated by a few mega egos who seem to be experts on *everything*.

The truth is, you do not know what a client is willing to pay unless they say, *"hey I'm only gonna pay $500"*. In which case you say, *"I can't help you,"* and move on and quickly.

You never want to do business with *price only buyers*. They are the bottom of the heap and will never appreciate your skills and product offering.

The good news is, it's just a small percentage of the population that buy only on best price.

But, if you are offering a commodotised service, then you can expect customers and clients to shop around for the best deal.

When I first left the security of a staff job back in 2001, I was a freelance television lighting cameraman. I was based in London where there was a fair bit of TV production work and I had a solid client base of broadcasters and independent production companies that would hire me on a day rate to shoot a variety of programmes.

I'd earn anywhere from £200 - £375 per 10 hr day, depending on the client and production. That was me without kit. Now, if I had a kit, I could charge more, but the trouble was that different clients wanted different formats and so I came 'as is', but I did have my own lighting kit, simply because I liked to light with certain tools and so it make my job easier. I also had a 7" wireless Director's monitor, that I'd rent to certain productions. I'd generally get £40 per day for that kit.

However, I was still *commodotised*.

Even though I had clients and directors who asked for me, I was still only one of a pool of possible cameramen who could shoot, and so the rates were set by production. My only influence was to say, *"yes"* or *"no"* to the gig. I had *no flexibility* on my rate of pay.

That is being commodotised. No matter how good I was, they were only going to pay a *set day rate* for a cameraman.

It's a bit like hiring a plumber or a domestic electrician - you are likely to shop around to get a recommendation, and then look for the best price, because if one is not available then you can always find another.

I had an interesting discussion with a production manager about five years ago, when she tried to hire me to come in and do some consulting for them. She wanted me to advise them on purchasing some location camera kits.

At that time, I'd increased my prices to £750 per day - and her words were, *"Blimey Den, when did you get so expensive? I can get a cameraman for £350."* She never hired me.

Now, this was a very important step in my career. Because I was worth it, and she did not see the value - so I did not do the job. But other clients were *very happy to pay that for me* to come in for a day and train their in house shooters.

The best bit was I actually hated dealing with the previous woman. She was all over you like a rash when she wanted something but never willing to pay, so I naturally *culled a crap client by pricing myself out of the bottom of the market*.

These can be tough decisions, but very important ones if you want to grow.

You have to get comfortable stepping outside your comfort zone.

It's very important to be *reassuringly expensive*. When you tell a client the price, and you don't wince a little at the bottom line figure, then you're *not charging enough*.

Price based buyers only ever look at the spend, and never the added value you can bring to their production.

Now, you have to be confident that you can add value and be willing to demonstrate that and back it up. But any good business relationship will offer you that opportunity.

The best relationship is one that allows you to solve problems for the client before they think of them. More on that in Chapter 8 - *How To Sell*.

The secondary effect of upping your prices is that it sends a message out to the price buyers... I have no doubt that the production manager who always wanted me cheap would have told all of her network, and the net result meant I did not have to waste any time on phone calls to clients who could not afford me. This saved me time and hassle and allowed me to focus on new clients who were willing to pay my higher rates. It was an important repositioning exercise that meant the market no longer saw me as a cameraman for hire at a predetermined rate.

Nowadays, my coaching rate starts at £1250.00 per day. That's a 400% increase on what I used to charge as a commodotised cameraman in less than six years. I did this simply by putting up my prices and focusing on a different end of the market. If I can do it, then so can you.

Know Your True Cost Of Doing Business

The biggest mistake I see creatives make is not factoring in the *true cost* of doing business.

Often I hear people discussing their day rates, and then in the same breath talk about buying some new gear because it's only X times their day rate, and so if they earn £300 per day and want to buy a new lens costing £900, then it's only three x a £300 day rate.

What they are *not factoring in* are all the associated costs of running their business.

All of the items below need to be factored into your *day rate* (if that's how you charge out your time).

Let's take a look at the kind of things I'm referring to:

- Upgrading equipment
- Computers and storage
- Electricity
- Rent & rates
- Accountancy fees
- Annual return fees
- Marketing costs
- Printing and other stationery costs
- Bank charges
- Equipment repair and maintenance
- Training & continuous improvement
- Memberships and associations
- Car costs, repayments, insurance, fuel
- Business insurance, public liability, employers liability
- Business coaching & personal development

Now, you may add more to this list and it's by no means definitive, but it does give you some insight into some of the associated costs with running a business. These things need to be paid for with something, and so if you are currently working on a *day rate for hire* model, then you need to look closely at all of those costs and add them together. Whatever that final number is, you need to divide by 12 and that's the monthly premium you need to cover to ensure you are actually turning a profit.

When you start to manage productions the *'Den Lennie Way'*, then you factor these costs into your *pre-production line items* and *production fees.* (More on that in chapter 3)

How much gear to buy

Buying *too much gear too soon* can cripple your cash flow and your business. Be careful.

The internet is awash with the latest and greatest tools and tech that you can easily justify to yourself as a business essential. But especially when starting out, you need to be very disciplined in what you buy. All too often I see filmmakers buying the wrong gear and then it sits on the shelf not turning a profit.

Here's my list of basic items that I regard as essential in running a video business:

- Camcorder, media and batteries
- 2-3 zoom lenses (in this order) Canon 17-55mm f2.8, Tokina 11-16mm f2.8, (Canon 70-200mm f4)
- Good fluid head tripod
- 2-3 head light kit
- Portable video monitor with waveform monitor built in
- Small portable slider
- Sound kit, boom, radio mic, lapel mic and headphones
- MacBook Pro for editing with FCPX or Premier Pro
- Raided hard drives for editing and archiving

Avoid focusing too much effort on your website

You might think this is an odd place to mention a website, but it's very important you hear me out on this. *You do not need to spend thousands on a website design in order to run a successful video production business.* Often when I talk to filmmakers starting out, they are obsessed with creating a show reel and building a website.

Websites are simply a digital business card, a virtual storefront if you like. When someone checks you out, the first thing they are likely to do is look at your website. It verifies that you are real. The reason it's important to highlight this here and not in the marketing chapters (which we will of course discuss in more detail in Chapter 5), is because web design can be a very costly and unnecessary expense.

My production business, until recently, did not have *any sort of web presence* and yet we were generating over six figures in revenue per year, on production.

I only recently built a basic site, and I did it myself in under four hours using Squarespace. It's a very basic four page website, which just has some work we've done and a few links. I don't even have all of the corporate work on there; I just put up the stuff I like to do so that if I meet someone who I'd like to create some content for, they can take a look at the type of projects we *specialise in.*

The key here is to specialise. I only put up content that I want to do more of. That way, by only showing niche work, we get known for it.

Remember, I spent less than *four hours of my time creating it* and it costs me $96 for 12 months. That's for everything.

On the other hand, I have spent over £30,000 having a bespoke website built for fstopacademy.com over the last three years. And it is always being upgraded and tweaked. Do I need it? Maybe, maybe not, but it's built now, so I am in a position to continue maintaining it, and I have something completely unique to me.

But if I had my time again, I'd probably just go with Squarespace and save a ton of money.

While on the subject of web design, I've come to realise it's so hard to find a great and reliable web designer. I've been through about four. Now I have a great team, but they are not cheap. (But then again, cheap and quality rarely go hand in hand.) And more importantly, I trust them and so the money is well spent.

But do be very wary of website designers. There are two key elements to website design; the look of the site (*the design*) and how it functions (*the coding*). After that comes the hosting.

I learned this lesson the hard way. It's very rare to find a great designer who is also a great coder. This is just my experience and I've spent a lot of money and time trying to get the right combination.

In fact, I got some advice early on in my business about web hosting. We had predicted a large amount of traffic and so went with an all singing all dancing dedicated server from Rackspace. It cost me over £750 per month in our first year of business. It was a small fortune, but I did not know any better and as a predominantly online business back then, I felt it was an important expense. *Wrong!* Not only did I lock into a 12 month contract, I spent *£9,000 on web hosting in our 2nd year in business*. This was a huge, not to mention expensive, mistake. In contrast, we now use a server costing £80 per month which is a big difference from £750. My annual hosting bill is now £960 per year - 10x less than my first server - but you live and learn; that's life!

The important thing for you is to *avoid the mistakes I made*. So by rights, that last paragraph alone just saved you **£8,000**... *pretty good return on investment for the cost of this book?*

Stick with something like Squarespace to begin with, because none of my video production work has come as a result of having a fancy website. Zero, nada, nowt.

Don't rent an office just yet…

Office space is another big no no when you are starting out. It's simply an unnecessary expense. Unless a client insists on sitting in on an edit, you can generally manage without rented office space.

In almost all cases, I edit the projects I produce remotely and deliver links to offline versions of an edit via *Vimeo*. When a client makes noises about wanting to sit in on an edit, I try to discourage them. Firstly, I don't want someone breathing down my neck as I form an edit; it's something I like to do in isolation and in silence. But secondly, I like to have the client see the first cut as a link. That way, they get to view the film as their intended audience might watch it - I think the viewing experience is better for the client this way.

Furthermore, if you have researched your project well and have done a solid pre-production job, then the edit should come together without the need for your client to be sat next to you dictating what shots you should use. Not only is it irritating, but often when a client gets sat behind an edit deck, they suddenly 'think' they are a filmmaker.

Avoid this - *set your process out for them from the outset* and remember it's *your* business, so *your* rules. You can explain that you like to craft the first cut alone, then deliver that to the client for consolidated feedback.

I digress - office space. You can run your business from a laptop, via email and by phone. I started F-Stop Academy from a wooden shed in my garden. In our third year of business, I had a builder double the size of the shed and now we have 20 sqm. Not huge but enough to house my edit and grading suite, a 65" 4k Bravia and some racks for gear. It's actually just big enough to shoot green screen in.

This year I actually started running out of space and so now rent a storage locker where I keep all my boxes, cases and heavy grip gear. But that's after five years in business, and I wanted more work space in the office because I like to brainstorm on large white boards, and I was just getting overrun with boxes and lighting stands.

Ironically, now that I'm paying £350 per month for storage, I'm wondering why I have all of this stuff. As a result I'm selling excess gear and getting rid of any heavy grip. I'm also scaling down my shooting package.

I've realised that for the limited corporate films I now shoot, I can do what I need with my Sony A7s, Kessler Stealth traveller and a Milller Compass 20. I have a comprehensive audio kit from Rode mics and some Sony digital radio mics. I have a simple lighting kit from F&V and I rent everything else for the bigger jobs. I do have a large amount of lenses, but that is more my passion than an absolute necessity.

My new approach is to have a shooting kit that fits comfortably in a Think Tank Airport Roller bag. That way you only need to be able to store it in a corner of your room and you don't need a whole office come storage space for cumbersome gear.

Small is beautiful.

Chapter 3
PRICING

How To Charge Premium Prices

"How much should I charge?" is probably the most commonly asked question I receive here at F-Stop Academy. And the answer is: as much as your client is willing to pay.

In business it is your duty to maximise your profit.

If you are offering a premier boutique video production service then *charge accordingly*. If you are going to go out into the marketplace and make beautiful films that help your clients sell more of their products, services or widgets then why not be the best and charge 5* prices?

I'm serious. If you're gonna go to the trouble of setting up a business and are putting yourself and your livelihood on the line, surely it makes sense to make as much money as you can?

The only caveat is that you are genuinely offering a superior service than your competitors.

Let me be clear. You cannot simply charge five star prices if you're only presenting yourself as a three star service. The value *has to be* of five star standards.

The secret here is to be very focused on your clients' problems and do everything you can to solve them, with the minimum of fuss.

If your client is say a marketing manager and has a team of fivepeople in their department then there's every likelihood that the project they have commissioned from you is only one project in five or more that they may be responsible for at any given time.

Here's how the client will be seeing the project:

- They need a video shooting
- They don't care about what camera you are using
- It needs to be on message
- It needs to fulfil the brief
- It needs to be delivered on time
- It needs to fit a predefined budget*
- It needs to work
- It needs to happen with minimal fuss
- It has to be shot on a certain day for various reasons
- Jane in another department has heard about the shoot and wants to film another product as part of it, seeing as they are already paying for a crew.

*This is often an arbitrary figure. There will be a provisional budget internally for what they want to assign to the project. In my experience, this can always be negotiated. Also once we begin to discuss a project the scope always grows. We refer to this as scope creep. The client will have a figure in mind that they want to spend and it's your job to upsell them to the point where you are offering so much value they are willing to spend more than they first planned to.

Most of all, the client wants a hassle free life. Most likely they will be a middle or senior manager on a salary. It's just one project of many that they may be looking after throughout the year. Your job is to take away their headaches and make life easy for them. Remove their pain and they will happily pay you for that.

We humans are extremely motivated away from pain. When you work in a corporation, the workload can be overbearing. I know because I've done it. When you get a chance to hire external suppliers this can really lighten your load, provide a good excuse to break the monotony and get out on a shoot. Do not underestimate the fun aspect of a client who gets to leave the daily grind and go on a film shoot. It's fun and exciting. Do not underestimate this value.

So, how do you package for a premium price?

Apple sell relatively expensive computers and laptops. I am a Mac user and, ever since buying my first Mac back in 2004, I've never looked back.

I love them. I love how easy they are to use, I love how cool they look, and I love the whole Apple experience.

And yet I can have a 'Hackintosh' built that will be more powerful and cheaper than the equivalent Mac. Technically better, and more processing and memory.

However, for me, it's about the packaging and experience.

I'm a creative; Macs are cool, PC's are not (just my opinion), and that is the basic crux of the marketing. Apple is a premium brand. I still pay £49 a year for my .mac email account - even though I have a Gmail account that I pay nothing for. I do this because I feel part of a club and I don't want to give it up. I might lose the email address (an example of avoiding the pain of loss), daft I know, but I cherish it enough to pay £49 per year for something I can get for no cost elsewhere.

Digging deeper into this, I realise that I am happy to pay top dollar for the new MacBook Pro Retina when it comes out. Even though I could have a more powerful machine if I switched to a PC that would likely cost me less.

But Apple present that machine to me, with its solid aluminium chassis, in its perfectly designed box; even the way they wrap the cable just oozes care and attention to detail.

That is premier positioning. That's what allows you to charge a premium for your product.

I like to be reassuringly expensive. It gives confidence to a client - but, like I said earlier - you have to be confident that you can deliver a premier product and service.

Why Charging For Every Service Is Critical

A big failing that I come across with filmmakers is – *"I'm a nice guy, so I don't charge for pre-production."*

What has being a nice guy and making money got to do with each other? You can still be a nice guy and make a profit.

I'm certain that you are not charging accordingly for all the services you offer.

Pre-production is a common 'forget to charge for' item.

Let's just consider some of the services that you could be currently providing to your clients, without actually charging a line item for.

Any of these ring a bell with you?

Pre-production Services

- Location research/scouting
- Developing a concept
- Emails/phone calls back and forward with client to discuss the project
- Creating project briefs, development and proposal documents
- Calling crew to check availability

- Coordinating gear
- Locating and securing props, costumes, hair and make up
- Budgeting and creating an estimate
- Revising the estimate if required
- Scheduling and planning the shoot days
- Scheduling post-production and booking edit facilities
- Revising scripts, concepts, creative briefs
- Securing insurance and liability quotes

The important thing to realise is that each of these tasks represents time; your time which is valuable as well as your experience and your contacts. Therefore, it should all be billed for and line itemised. Now, in practice, I don't line itemise everything I've just listed. Rather I bundle it under pre-production fees. Then if a client asks for an explanation I list the tasks as above - and now you can too.

Rates for pre-production are determined by the scale and duration of the overall project. For example, a one-day shoot may only require a half day of prep, but a week long foreign location shoot with two separate films to cut and multiple locations could have two to four weeks of pre-production preparation.

I also usually charge a week for post-production (admin and management) on larger jobs. Simply because of what I referred to earlier as scope creep. This is a fee that covers all of the post-production administration from a larger project. Goal posts always get moved during post-production. Relatively small changes and extra versions may on the surface seem slight, but each non planned change requires time to remaster or make changes. There can often be an ongoing dialogue with the client at this stage and this can be time consuming.

I have had clients say one thing during production and then do a 180 in post and we end up recutting an item. The facts are that even with the greatest relationships and planning, things change and you need to factor that into your budget so you do not end up pissed off and out of pocket.

How to present an estimate

Presenting your estimate in the right way is *vital* to how your client perceives the final figure.

Let's be honest, video production can get expensive, but when you are a corporate manager and you are not expecting the big number it can really shock you. Let's say the client has only ever made a few short videos before, but they've decide they need something more professional. Nothing will prepare them for the true cost of quality: especially if they are used to only doing print ads and editorial. Having a writer create some copy or a designer to design a flyer is relatively inexpensive. Even a top designer may only charge £300 per day, and a writer the same.

But when you start factoring in equipment, location costs, travel and crew, the costs can suddenly be up into the multiple thousands before too long. The client may not fully understand the process and so will potentially fall off their chair if you just launch a figure at them.

It's your job to educate them and help them understand your process so they can grasp why each element has a cost associated with it.

Also, corporate companies tend to be very administrative heavy-expenses and other internal financial procedures can be very systemised. I remember when I was staff at the BBC, the bureaucracy was off the scale. But I learned a valuable lesson. Corporate clients like to know what each line item does because then they can assign a code. By presenting your estimate as line items and assigning a code it already makes sense to them. They are on familiar ground.

So that's exactly how I lay out my estimates. I break down and line itemise the process.

Begin by splitting the estimate into 3 sections

1. Pre-production

2. Production

3. Post-production

This clearly splits the filmmaking process up into three distinct stages so that the client understands that there are individual stages that all have a number of processes, each of which has to be carried out by someone and therefore has a tangible cost attached to it.

I then break each stage of production down into its component parts. (Below is an example.)

1. Pre-production

(Includes any or all of the relevant items in *Pre-production services* listed on page 54/55.)

2. Production

(This can include any of the following.)

- Camera hire
- Lighting hire
- DOP/cameraman
- Camera assistant
- Sound recordist
- Grip equipment hire
- Director
- Producer
- Travel

- Hotels
- Subsistence (Craft Services in USA)
- Parking and tolls
- Location fees
- Permits
- Digital storage (SSDs, HDDs & memory)
- Hair & make-up
- Production assistant
- Production runner
- Talent costs
- Production insurance
- Contingency
- Set/expendables

As for exactly how much to charge for each of the above services, well that is largely dependent on how experienced the personnel you hire are and the nature of the project. Crew rates fall within certain categories. For example BECTU in the UK (the media and entertainment union with some 25,000 memberships to negotiate rates across broadcast and production companies) have a list of their agreed day rates for certain types of production, see https://www.bectu.org.uk/advice-resources/rates

In my experience, BECTU tend to cater more for the film industry and commercials, whereas with corporate video production it is not so easy to pin down an exact rate. These rates are only guidelines anyway.

▣ I've put together a guide table over at www.businessforfilmmakers.com/rates, but please use this only as a guide. Every client and job can be different and there is simply no 'one size fits all'.

3. Post-production

- Media ingest and logging
- Offline edit suite hire
- Online edit suite hire
- Offline editor
- Online editor
- Grading suite hire per hour
- Colourist
- Graphics
- Music composition/licence
- Sound mix
- Exports and renders
- Media and Archiving

You may be surprised to learn that post-production can eat up a large part of any production estimate.

I recall talking with a production manager many years ago who was looking after a 12x30 min TV series, and she said the largest portion of her budget went on post. Therefore, it is very important that you fully set out all of the different steps involved in post producing, even on the smallest corporate video.

Remember, you are providing a professional service and so everything you do to make that film happen has a time/resource attached to it and should be charged for.

I'm going to break down each section and elaborate to give you a better understanding of what is involved, which in turn will help you to explain it all to your client. That way, you educate your client and they understand why post costs are what they are.

Media ingest & logging

If you shoot six hours of footage on a shoot day then that is going to take anywhere between two to six hours to ingests and transcode. With so many different video formats now available, and several editing platforms, there will generally be some type of conversion required and this eats into your post schedule. Take GoPro footage, for example. I use the GoPro Studio app to import footage shot on my DJI Phantom and convert it from the 2.5k format to 1920x1080. I also use the inbuilt features to remove the fish eye from the lens. Then I export it into Quicktime ready for ingest into FCPX. Now this is not a quick process, and despite me having a top spec MacPro, it still takes time.

This one example, and I'm sure you have a different workflow. Now, back in the days of tape, post houses generated massive revenue for what they called ingest and transcode. This was in some cases £90 per hour and was a real time process where a junior tape operator would load in tapes and import the footage in real time to the NLE (nonlinear editor).

Nowadays, we may be working with media files, but there are still time implications to get the footage imported and all talking the same language on the timeline.

Don't forget, you are running a business and so if you have invested in a high powered machine that will make this process faster, that should be a benefit to you and not the client, e.g you charge an hourly rate for ingest and if you can do it faster, then you can take on more jobs simultaneously if you choose. Any capital spend on infrastructure has to be paid for by someone, and so be aware of what your system upgrades have cost you. Build that into your overall post facilities fee.

Offline edit suite & offline editor

In practice, you may choose to charge out offline editing as a package that includes the suite and the editor. But it is important to understand that there are two parts to the offline process.

Facility hire and an offline editor (the talent)

Offline editing is a hangover from the days of tape when the ingested footage was stored at a lower resolution for speed of working, and so all of the edit decisions were made on a low resolution copy of the files. Once a picture lock was agreed then the online editor would relink the low res files with the full res originals and sync everything up.

Certainly much of what I'm sharing with you can be performed on a laptop these days, and often we'll work at full native resolution. But while I can and do edit on my laptop when I have to, I prefer to ingest everything into my main suite if I can. The reason is that I have faster storage in my suite. I use a mixture of G-Tech G-Drives set to Raid 0 for speed and Promise Technology Pegasus R6 for security set to Raid 5.

I also have a 34" 21x9 LG screen, and a TV Logic Grade 1 24" reference monitor that also feeds a 65"4K Sony Bravia. Now I'm not suggesting you need this level of monitoring, but much of our corporate work involves producing launch film for manufacturers in the film and video arena, and so we need to have critical monitoring up to 4k. You simply cannot view critical footage on a 15" laptop screen. But mostly this set up is for my online and grading work.

I have probably spent around £30-35k on my main edit and grading suite, and in order for that to be a viable investment, I need to be making sure that every project is paying off a chunk of the investment and allowing for profit margin on top.

I charge offline editing at a day rate for 10 hours, and this includes hire of the suite and the offline editor. When quoting I make an educated assessment of how long I think the edit will take and also factor in time for changes.

So, if I've shot a straight forward one day project and the client wants a three min cut film, I'd usually budget for three days of offline. That would allow time for the ingest and review of footage, first cut and second round of modifications. Beyond that, I'd bill additional days. Remember, an estimate is just that. Be sure when you present your estimate to explain that there may be scope creep and changes that take the edit beyond the three days estimated.

Online editing and editor

While the technical requirement from offline to online may be less significant today, there are still distinct processes that differ between offline and online editing. For example, when cutting the offline, the client does not really need to be paying for the 10K broadcast grade one monitor or the 4k Bravia because for the purposes of making edit decisions the computer screen is more than adequate and so the offline rental rates should be lower than online.

When online editing you are making sure that everything is up to the quality required for final delivery. This is when you need to be using a high quality grade one production monitor, and if delivering 4K then you need to be monitoring to a 4K display.

I charge out online editing on an hourly basis and include the suite and the editor. If we use the example of the three minute film I'd probably charge four hours of online. I tend to work at native resolution and so do not need to relink to high res files, which saves me a process. I factor in time because the way I am able to do that is by investing in larger and faster thunderbolt raid storage which means I have greater capacity for larger files.

The online process is also where I charge for the renders and exports and any multiple versioning that the client requires.

Once the online work has been completed, I move on to the grade.

Grading & colourist

This is a relatively new service I've been offering (for the last 18 months or so). With so many cameras now shooting on a log mode, grading becomes essential in the process. But most clients don't know what it is and so you have to educate them.

Using something like Magic Bullet Looks will go some way to giving an overall wash of colour correction to your film. It's a bit like taking a large brush and affecting everything in the scene.

The trouble is, you affect everything in the scene, so if you wanted to give a cool wash to your shot then even the skin tones would go blue. With proper grading using DaVinci Resolve Lite (which is free see www.businessforfilmmakers.com/resources) you can isolate any part of the scene and apply a different correction or grade. When selling grading to clients, I show them before and after shots to help them see the value. It's also very important if you are doing any work with brands which have a specific corporate colour palette that must be accurate.

This is when having a calibrated video monitor (that is not your computer screen) is vital.

No matter how well you shoot a project, there will always be shots that don't match for various reasons. Typically, just changing camera angles can result in light looking different from one shot to another. Colour grading in its first instance is used to correct and match shots on a sequence.

Grading can be an additional revenue stream for you. I charge an hourly rate for grading that includes the colourist and the suite hire.

Obviously you have to learn how to colour grade if you are going to offer this service yourself, but if not then you can subcontract the grading and still offer it to your client. There are some free tutorials over at www.businessforfilmmakers.com/resources to help you get started with grading in DaVinci Resolve.

Graphics

Graphics and titles are technically part of the online process in my book, but depending on the complexity of the work you may choose to farm it out to a graphic designer. I use Final Cut X and Apple Motion, so in most cases I can handle the graphics in house, but occasionally I'll get someone else involved if it is beyond my capability. Once the graphics have been created, they then need to be inserted and this falls under online editing in my business and so is factored into the hourly charge for online.

Music licence, composition & sound mix

If you are producing work for commercial purposes and you use music then you are legally obliged to pay for the licence and usage. I use a music library and the services of composers, depending on the project.

I typically add the music during online time, but the licence fees vary depending on duration, usage and number of tracks used. I use a music library called Audio Network and I pay an annual licence fee for unlimited usage worldwide. I then charge my client on usage of music.

The crux of this involves me paying for the annual licence upfront, then marking up any tracks used to the client. This provides a good way of generating additional revenue during a project.

Media & archiving

This is an often missed opportunity for your profit margin. When a project is complete, I offload it to LTO tape. This is Data tape that has a 30 year archival shelf life.

The infrastructure to work with LTO costs me about £2,500, with the hardware and software and ach LTO 5 tape, which holds 1.6TB of uncompressed data, costing me about £20.

But what you can offer is a secure backup and archive of the client's work. Storing long term on hard drives gets expensive and risky. Hard drives fail. LTO is much safer.

So, not only can you charge out a line item for the archiving process and tape, but you then have the client in a place where they need to come back to you if they want any recuts or new edits.

I had a client recently call us 18 months after the initial job needed some footage for a TV broadcast. I was able to charge them £250 to retrieve the footage from archive, burn it to hard drive and ship it to the BBC. The BBC then sent me back the drive. So you should always consider the long term value of a client and the resources you create. The added benefit here is that you sell it to them as a safety net. That way you are helping them protect their assets while ring fencing them as a customer. Never ever give them the rushes (the raw, unedited footage). They will never come back to you and someone new will come into the office and say they have a mate who can edit... boom, gone forever.

Remember, you're in business to make money, not new friends. Sure, business relationships can be friendly, but protect your assets at all times. There are untapped profits in your archive.

One thing to remember is that when you are commissioned to make a film for a client, you are paid to deliver a finished edit. The client does not own the footage unless they explicitly make that part of the deal up front.

Don't Discount - Add Value

Some clients will always ask for a discount. Some people have the mentality, *"if you don't ask you don't get"*. For many it's just a desire to feel like they've flexed their muscles and got a deal.

I generally try to avoid discounting - that is to say, giving away real money. There is a way to demonstrate discounts that are, to all intents and purposes, virtual discounts. I usually add a covering letter to a quote and show any discounts on the actual estimate too.

Here's an example of a covering letter I sent to a client a few years ago. (I've changed the names for the sake of confidentiality.)

Hi Jeremy

I've now had several meetings with Donald about how we can make this project really stand out and give you the training elements required, but also produce a very glossy, 'high perceived value' product to help support and drive the sales of the product across Europe.

This project has been priced up now and the quote is coming in higher than the cursory figures I gave you verbally yesterday. Although actual production costs are in line with the figures we discussed.

By adding contributor fees, Blu-ray authoring, design and packaging, etc. the costs have grown. However, all of these costs are detailed on the next page.

Donald and I will collaborate creatively on this project, we have also agreed not to charge a fee for our participation in the interviews portion that we are producing.

In addition, we've not charged for camera hire or additional lighting sound and grip in lieu of the equipment you have supplied. This combined demonstrates a real saving of £5,900 to you. We're happy to do this as we enjoy working with you and wish this project to be the beginning of bigger things for us all.

In terms of other savings, Donald has reduced the directing fee by 80% as he will make his margin up on the post production of this project.

I'm charging a producing fee, but within that I will also DP the shoots and Donald and I will both film the content together. This further reduced the requirement for a cameraman, saving another £2625. We've also removed the sound recordist fee as we'll manage that ourselves on this component, saving another £2450. So, all in all we've been able to reduce the overall production costs by £10,975.

The costs overleaf include all production of the 60 minute 'Profile & tips' aspect and the inclusion of the 'round table' aspect being produced by your other agency. They will just need to deliver a colour corrected, cut 30 minute master and we'll add the graphics and include it online, then prepare the transcription and liaise with the translations (done by your in house team) build all the components for the Blu-ray and get that all manufactured so you will receive 1000 *finished products. N.B. the price quoted for Blu-ray is Duplication. If you wish to go beyond 1000 units we should consider Replication which involves creating a glass master then printing the units. But we have contingency in the budget for that.*

The Total Production Budget is £50,190 - all broken down on the next page. Perhaps you can give me a call once you've digested it and we can discuss the next steps.

Den

I always include a covering letter that details where we have made economies prior to the first estimate being sent to the client. The psychology behind this is to demonstrate that a large amount of work and consideration has already been done. This makes it harder for a client to then ask for further discount. If they do you simply refer them back to your letter, where you have already discounted.

▣   If you'd like to view the actual estimate then you can see it over at www.businessforfilmmakers.com/exampleestimate

What to do when the client says *"Your quote is too expensive!"*

If you are pricing correctly then at some point a client may say, *"your estimate is too expensive, we need to reduce it".*

What do you do, and more importantly, how do you do it?

Firstly, it's entirely up to you if you want to drop your trousers and give them a discounted rate. The trouble with this approach is that they will think you were trying it on in the first place. This is not a solution I recommend.

A more intelligent approach is to suggest to the client that you go back over the estimate together and see what elements are less important in order to reduce costs. For example, cutting a shoot day and resulting edit days. But obviously in doing so, you won't be able to make the film that they hope for with a reduction in shoot days.

Or perhaps they'd like to cut down the number of locations and maybe save on a location fee?

You see where I'm going with this don't you? If they want to save money then you have to start streamlining the shoot, which will result in them getting less of a film.

The only way to save money on your estimate is by reducing the scale of the project. If the client really needs to bring it in cheaper, then they have to be realistic about their expectations. If they want to cut the budget then you need to cut back on the shoot. It's simple. Otherwise you are reducing your profit margin for no reward.

The exception I allow is for faster payment. If someone wants a reduction so the estimate fits a number they had set aside, then I'll often say OK, but payment up front or by a designated date.

For a deal to work, both parties need to feel good about it;
it has to be a win-win deal.

Make sure you charge for the creative concept

This is something that many filmmakers find hard to do. But it is an important part of a project. Now, it's not necessarily something that every job needs. But for larger productions where I have been commissioned to conceive and produce a project, I will put a line item in the budget for creative development. Creativity is a skill we filmmakers have and it becomes an important part of the production and so should be chargeable. Otherwise, where do the ideas come from?

Now, it really depends on the production as to how I factor these costs in. As I mentioned on a large end to end production like a DVD, I'll include an actual line item in the estimate. But on smaller productions, it's harder to justify to a client and so I just factor in an extra week of pre-production or equivalent to cover the time taken to conceive, nurture and develop an idea. Sometimes in these cases I'll factor in extra pre-production days for the producer and director to allow for the idea development.

Charging a Production Fee (& Contingency Planning)

In broadcast television, when a production company is awarded a series it's common for them to charge a production company fee. This is usually 12.5 to 15% of the overall budget. If you have an infrastructure that involves office space, full time staff and administrative support, I think it can easily be justified. Another example is when you take on a large project that will require a lot of day-to-day admin.

In fact, I had a client question the production fee on a job last year and here's how I responded to that email.

"The production company fee is an administration fee and covers many things that are not line itemised.

I'll try to explain:

Line itemised costs are specific costs particular to the exact shooting days and hard production costs. However, on top of that the production company has an office overhead: light, power, administration staff and support, telephone, internet, bank and credit card charges, Forex charges, banking costs when employing a team of productions staff, processing and paying of accounts, invoices, equipment maintenance/depreciation of gear we own and use on every shoot over and above cameras.

The production fee is a % fee that is charged on every production, regardless of size. It covers experience, contacts, relationships we might have with suppliers that get a better deal for you on certain production items, and things like time spent developing quotes and researching. It covers making bookings, production management, production co-ordination, making call sheets, preparing all legal and insurance paperwork, getting licences and location release paperwork, and other such non line itemised parts of a production process.

Also, when we raise invoice in €, the day we make the transfer our bank will charge a rate of exchange, and, as all of our production costs are in £ we need to factor in this also as a 0.% change in conversion can cost hundreds of €.

Normally production fees can range from 15% to 30% and so I wanted to make you a good deal at 12%."

Client response: "I also understand production fee. Of course we do have those kinds of costs here as well."

I continued....

"You will notice that we are not charging for camera kit hire, matte box hire, tripod hire, sound gear, on set monitoring...these are our basic kit items that we include in our production fee, but still have an overall cost to our production company.

Unfortunately, the line items are specific costs we estimate.

Hope that makes sense.

Oh, and the Production Contingency is a % of 'overages' - by this I mean, when we prepare a budget it is that - just an estimate of costs. Things always cost more than expected in film production. E.g parking costs are higher, extra lighting is needed in a particular location, more set dressing is needed. Having contingency as part of the production budget allows us to have some flexibility.

An example would be the shoot I have just finished in Istanbul. I had budgeted €800 for a location fixer, but when we came to it the fixer was actually €1050. Then we had €750 on costs for permits that were not expected. We cannot predict all costs upfront and so in order to sign off on a budget we include a 10% contingency that almost always gets absorbed in actual production costs. Another example was that we needed to rent two boats to film for 1 hr - The company initially suggested €200 but on the day , these boats were broken and we had *to take bigger ones costing €400. By the time everyone is on set, we have to make a decision to keep shooting and accept the extra costs… but they were impossible to budget for, so our line items are real costs with the contingency in place to make up any shortfall."*

Client Response: *"I know and understand that you need a buffer to cover unexpected costs - of course some extra costs might appear."*

"Again, I hope that make this charge more clear."

Client Response: *"Thanks for your explanatory notes. It makes it clearer for me."*

So as you can see it's all about *educating the clients clearly,* explaining why certain costs exist.

Contingency fee or production overages?

The final line item I want to discuss is the *contingency fee* or production overages, as its sometimes called.

I referred to it in the email above.

In simple terms, estimates are just that; you can never fully prepare for actual expenses on location. It's just impossible and costs always add up, and never the other way around. The contingency fee is usually 10% or the production element of the budget. It is there to protect you and give the client a bottom line figure that they know will not increase. By including contingency in the estimate you are factoring in a financial buffer. It's also impossible to get receipts for every expense on production. Parking meters, for example, don't issue receipts, and sometimes you need to pay someone in cash to gain access to a location. It's the nature of production and so you need to explain that to your client.

Chapter 4
GETTING THINGS DONE

Right Brain vs Left Brain Tasks

I am no psychologist or scientist, but in order to better understand how you prioritise and manage different tasks, I'm going to draw on *right brain* vs *left brain* concepts commonly discussed in science.

In simple terms, it's widely believed that we have a dominance towards one side of the brain's ability to process information.

It's often said that you are either more left brain focused or right brain focused.

Right brain tends to lean towards *creativity*:

- Recognising faces
- Expressing emotions
- Music
- Reading emotions
- Colour
- Images
- Intuition

Left brain dominance tends to prioritise more *logical thinking*:

- Language
- Logic
- Critical thinking
- Numbers
- Reasoning

In truth, I don't believe it is as cut and dry as that, but certainly there are tendencies that I lean towards. I'm naturally more right brained than left. That is to say I find *right brained tasks come more naturally to me.* As such, I tend to gravitate more easily to those daily projects that require my attention.

> *The trouble is that the nuts and bolts of running a business involve a good part of left brained thinking and application.*

I am naturally a daydreamer. If I have a task to complete that is left brained, I could easily find a dozen things to do other than the task in hand. Take completing expense forms as a prime example. I detest filling out spreadsheets. I hate it with a vengeance; I cannot get my head around Excel and how to set up equations to make one cell connect to another and apply rules. This drives me completely nuts. I therefore tend to ignore those tasks until I absolutely have to do them. (Actually, these days I have a bookkeeper who looks after all of that for me, but I'll come back to outsourcing later.)

My point is this; you will naturally lean one way or the other, so if you are right brained then you'll naturally migrate to those tasks and potentially *ignore* the left brained ones. At the very least you will feel greater resistance to those tasks. I know I do.

The trouble is, if you ignore the admin and financial tasks in your business, then you'll end up in all sorts of bother. You'll become more stressed, and if you miss a payment to the taxation department you'll be in a whole lot of trouble too.

We naturally tend to avoid pain as humans... And doing tasks that don't come easily or involve stepping out of our comfort zone takes effort. It's not easy. In fact, it can feel very painful.

There is a way you can make life easier for yourself. Firstly you have to realise *when* you are avoiding a task, then you *put a system in place* to make sure the job gets done with the minimum of resistance.

I am going to show you how I overcame these obstacles and share with you my principles for getting stuff done.

Self Discipline (JFDI)

So, there is no easy way to say this... but you are gonna have to get hardcore on yourself.

I will be sharing the apps and processes I use to help me achieve more but in essence you have to just get on with it. That means turning off email, ignoring social media and switching off your phone in order to get the mental space to deal with the task in hand.

Here are some things you can do to help;

We are most productive during the first two hours of any day; in fact, it has been suggested that you achieve more in the first twohours of every day than the rest of the day combined.

We are also cyclical; a mentor of mine, the marketer and business coach Eben Pagan, has taught me that we work most effectively in 45 minute bursts. In fact, he suggests using a stopwatch to time 45 minute bursts of focused activity, followed by a 10 to 15 minute break where you get up and walk around and drink some water before settling down to start another 45 minute burst.

I personally find this regimentation hard to follow, but I do take aspects and follow it in principle.

Turn off email; This is very, very important. When someone emails you, they have a deadline, not you. If you check your email every five minutes, then something can drop into your inbox and take your focus off what you were doing. It distracts you buy engaging you in another person's problem.

The world does not stop spinning because you don't reply to an email straight away. Email can become a form of instant messaging to some, and it sucks your productivity and more importantly your focus.

Here's what I do with my email; I have an auto reply set up, and it reads very simply:

Thank you for your message.

I check and respond to email twice daily at 12.00 P.M (GMT) and 4.00 P.M. (GMT)

Warmly

Den Lennie

It's a very effective way of letting people know politely, but firmly, that you are busy and will get back to them in due course. It also means you can be selective and prioritise the emails that need to be responded to first.

Do one more thing; either shut down your mail app altogether or at least turn off the alerts.

Same goes for your phone; stick it into airplane mode.

I am old enough to remember a world without mobile phones... we still managed to run businesses and manage our lives.

In fact, people were generally more punctual because they couldn't call or text to say they were running late. But I digress.

Turn off social media; another time and focus destroyer.

If you do choose to engage in social media, then limit it to twice per day and only if there are solid business reasons for it. I don't focus a lot of time or effort on social media. I think it's very time consuming and very hard to measure. There are many more things you can do with your time to market you and your business that have far greater returns than social media, but more on that in Chapter 5.

You might find this difficult to begin with and don't worry, like breaking any habit your brain does everything it can to return to the place of most comfort. Stick with it and be disciplined. It can take 30 to 60 days to break a habit and form a new one, so don't give up. If you want to become more efficient and get those opposite side brained tasks accomplished then you just need to do it.

My moto is JFDI 'Just Fucking Do It'.

Take writing this book as an example. I have to make myself write. I am not a natural writer. In fact, I chose not to do a 4th year at university and get my honours degree purely because I would have had to have written a 10,000 word dissertation How ironic that I'm now on course to write in excess of 60,000 words for this book.

So what changed? Well, maturity for one, and having a very clear goal that will help elevate me and my business to the next level.

This book is the backbone of my coaching business. My plan is to generate a percentage of revenue each year from working closely with filmmakers who want to grow their production business to $100,000 and beyond.

Writing a book means I become an author on the subject. I am the only person ever to have written a book dedicated to helping filmmakers grow in their business and marketing skills, and so by default I will become the world's leading authority on the subject. Because if you write a book on any subject, you instantly become an authority. But you have to know what you are talking about. And I do. I've been in the media industry since the age of 16, and have started a video production business from scratch with no external funding. I've grown it to multiple six figures in only five years. Importantly, this is not theory learned at business school. I've rolled up my sleeves, had an idea and worked very hard to make it a reality. In doing so, I have learned a massive amount along the way that I am now sharing with you in this book.

Some of you reading this book will go on to join my *Business For Filmmakers Inner Circle* and some of you will become private coaching clients as part of my Elite group. So, by writing a book and you reading it one of 4 things will happen.

1) You'll read it cover to cover, then read it again taking furious notes and implementing everything I suggest, seeing your business and bank balance grow.

2) You'll read it, and realise implementation is harder to achieve alone and join the Inner Circle, where a community of like-minded filmmakers from around the world get ongoing remote support from me and the other members in the group. After all having a platform to share your growth behind a closed door can really accelerate your development

3) You'll be a high achiever who needs more than a group environment and wants to work with me more closely to help take your business to where it needs to be in 12 to 18 months or less.

4) You'll get part of the way through the book, convince yourself that this is all nonsense and carry on as before bitching about clients and why they won't pay. And if that is you. contact my office and we'll refund you in full and you can even keep the book because you need all the help you can get.

My prediction is that around 15 to 20% of the readers of this book will take action and most likely join my Inner Circle. Then 3 to 5% will take it to the next level and apply to join my Elite coaching group. I say apply because you can't just join, you have to fulfil the criteria. But more on that later.

Either way, the only person any of the above decisions will truly affect is you. By reading this book, you are raising your hand and acknowledging that you need help, and that is a good thing. But simply reading this alone will not get you the results you want. You have to roll your sleeves up, make many sacrifices and do the graft.

But it is worth it if you can stay the distance. Because if you have the true desire and commitment to do what most people are not prepared to do, then you will achieve the freedom that no one else will be able to have in five years from now. Freedom is everything and it is within your grasp - freedom is a choice, as is financial secruity.

Productivity (tools)

There are countless productivity tools available, from apps to monthly subscriptions. These will largely come down to personal preference because everyone handles time management and to do lists differently.

The important thing is to get organised.

If you are anything like me, this is something that may take some discipline. I have to give credit to James Tonkin here from hangmanstudios.com, because he really demonstrated the true value of being super organised. James has run a boutique post-production company in London for over 12 years and is almost OCD when it comes to being organised. He attributes this to starting life as an editor. I've noticed that editors tend to be far more organised than camera people... Something to do with having hours of footage in a project that will send you loopy if you're not organised.

Productivity Apps; Evernote. The big discovery for me (via James) was *Evernote* (all the details can be found at www.businessforfilmmakers.com/resources)

I now cannot imagine running my business or life without Evernote. It's a digital workspace that allows me to make notes, scan documents directly into it (using a Fujistu Scanner - details on resources link above), store images, and keep a track of it all by using text recognition. You can search by a keyword and it will display all the documents you have with that related keyword. This is especially useful as I can create a folder for different aspects of my life. For example, I have a client folder, and when a particular client has a quote in process, or a request for a project, I store everything in that folder. This becomes useful for when a repeat client returns and I want to refer back to the previous jobs estimate and see what rates we were charging.

The really neat feature about Evernote is that it is cloud based and so everything is stored securely and you can sync it with your phone, iPad or desktop machines; everything then auto syncs.

I've become increasingly attached to cloud based applications. In the last year I have travelled extensively. Australia, New Zealand, Singapore, Ireland, Japan, Canada, Costa Rica, USA, Australia (again), Singapore (again), Hong Kong, Malaysia, Japan (again) and Dubai. I have to be able to run my business regardless of whether or not I am in the office.

Like I mentioned in Chapter 2, you don't need a brick and mortar office, but you do need all the important tools of a virtual office.

Create a weekly 'To Do' list. Another way I use Evernote is to create a *weekly 'to do' list*. I set my agenda at the beginning of the week (often adding to it as I go), and then simply tick stuff off as it gets done. I find this simple to do list invaluable for getting the tasks done. It's quite satisfying checking in at the end of the week and seeing all the stuff you've achieved.

Other services I rely on are **Dropbox, Google Drive, iCloud, Infusion Soft, Crazy Egg** and **Optimizely.**

Dropbox is cloud based file storage, which again syncs across my devices. I now have 5GB of storage, which is tons. I have all my important files backed up and they are easily accessible from any device from anywhere with an internet connection.

Google Drive is amazing. I am writing this book in Google Drive, its got a word app and a spreadsheet app as well as lots of other features like Google Mail and Google Calendar. I do all my shoot planning, quoting and budgets on the spreadsheet apps on Google Drive.

iCloud is useful, although I tend to use it more for personal stuff than business.

Infusionsoft is something I'll talk more about in Chapter 5 - but it is incredible. Now, for most of you it will be overkill unless you are planning to create content and sell it to a large database of people. Infusionsoft is my email delivery auto responder, it's my shopping cart and it's my CRM (customer relationship management) database software. It also does way more, but I use it primarily for those three purposes. I'll be talking more about email auto responders in the marketing chapters.

Crazy Egg is heat map software. This is very useful for tracking what visitors actually click on and mouse over on your website. It shows you exactly where people are clicking and where they come from. I've found this very useful for naming my navigation tabs on the top of my website at www.fstopacademy.com and also for improving the user experience. You can see an example of heatmap software at www.businesforfilmmakers.com/heatmap. It takes the guess work out of what people respond to more when they are on your site. It's part of optimising your site for maximum response.

Optimizely is another piece of analytics software that helps you to optimise the responsiveness and effectiveness of your website.

This works by creating split test variants of content and elements of your web page. For example, I split test the colour of the opt-in box on our website at www.fstopacacademy.com. We alternated what each visitor would see over a period of time to see what version performed better. This is called A/B split testing and we discovered that by changing the colour from red to orange we achieved a 6% increase in sign ups, simply by changing the colour of the box. When you begin to focus more on your marketing then this kind of detail becomes very important.

Outsourcing For Maximum Efficiency

We filmmakers are very adept at wearing many hats. Producer, director, editor, cameraman, sound… it's the nature of boutique production. It can mean that you can make more money by doing more of the jobs yourself, but equally it can thin your resources out a little finely.

There are certain jobs you will choose to do because you enjoy them, and that is perfectly fine. But I'm certain that you are still doing tasks that could easily be done by someone else if you paid them.

This is all about focusing on your high value tasks.

Do you do your own bookkeeping? Because you shouldn't be. I pay my bookkeeper £15 per hour and it costs me between £200 to 300 per month. That's 14 to 20 hrs per month that a full time trained bookkeeper takes to manage our monthly accounts, manage all of our VAT and keep a line by line track of every item of income and expenditure. This makes the end of year accounting much more efficient, plus we can track our monthly profit and loss and therefore estimate our tax liability as we go through the year, allowing us to factor in putting aside enough money for tax when it becomes liable.

It really doesn't make sense for you to do your own bookkeeping. It makes far more sense that you spend that time creating new marketing, communicating with existing customers, sending new prospects and existing customers any number of marketing messages to help remind them that you should be their number one trusted advisor and supplier of high quality video.

Perhaps you are a skilled producer and shooter. Working in these roles is more lucrative than, say offline editing. If you find a great editor you can spend more time producing and shooting and have someone else edit for you. The additional benefit of working with other creatives is the added creativity that will find its way into your work. Rodney Charters ASC said to me once: *"Filmmaking is not a solo pursuit it's about working with a team of talented individuals who collectively pool their knowledge, experience and resources to create something that is greater than the sum of all the parts."*

I even outsource camerawork these days. I do what I love, which is to produce and to light. I still wear the DP hat because I still take responsibility for the overall look and the lighting decisions on set. But somebody else sets the lights and somebody else operates the camera. That way we become more efficient.

I am also comfortable enough with my own ability and experience to let others into the mix and to add their angle on things. It makes the work better. I don't have to do everything myself.

Delegation and outsourcing are key, if you want to grow.

While we're on outsourcing, you can also hire external companies to answer your phone, take messages and act as a receptionist or PA (or a full secretarial service depending on the size and scale of your operation). This just emphasises the fact that you do not need an actual office and loads of staff to have all the benefits of a team.

Working weekends

In the early days you are going to be working seven days... no two ways about it. The sheer effort required to get the business off the ground will be at times overwhelming. There will be nights when you wake up in a panic wondering where the next job is gonna come from. I remember it all too well. But it's those moments that force you to dig deep and really work out what your next move will be. If you don't feel the pain of wondering how the mortgage will get paid next month, you never truly develop as a business owner. It's not easy; it's *really, really* hard at times. If it was easy everyone would do it. That's why people take the security of a staff job with a set reliable monthly income. It's safe.

But if you want to reap the rewards and the freedom that running your own boutique video business brings then you have to take the rough with the smooth. It's what toughens you up when you set your pricing higher than you are comfortable with. It's how you grow, and one day it all falls into place and suddenly you are earning more than you ever dreamed of.

I found an old payslip recently from only five years ago, and I was taking home £3195 per month. Today I was booked to do four one day presentations and my charge is £4200. So, to put that in perspective, five years ago I would have had to go to an office every day, five days per week, travel 1.5 hours each way to earn that money. Five years on, I do four days and earn more... That is freedom and progress. But it didn't happen on its own or by accident.

Don't do it alone

You don't have to do all of this alone. The best and most effective way to succeed is to model yourself on another successful person. That's why athletes have coaches, they need someone looking from the outside in to spot where small adjustments need to be made in order to maximise results.

Great singers still work with vocal coaches to maintain their voice and optimise their performance. Great actors work with acting coaches to refine their performance.

Having a coach is not new and if you want to achieve results that exceed your own expectations, then you should work with a coach. Now whether that's me or someone else - your choice - but it will become increasingly important as your business grows.

I have been hiring coaches for the last three years. I invest in them because they don't cost me a thing (any fees I've invsted have come back to me multi times over in increased profits). See, if you take the advice of a coach and apply the advice and implement the suggestions they make, your business will grow faster and greater than it would do, on its own.

I worked with one coach for 18 months; during that time he helped me to see my true value and worth. In that time I increased my shooting rates (when I was still shooting) from £350 per day to £950 per day - I practically tripled my fees. Sure, I hit some resistance, but I also had new clients who were more than happy to pay.

I am still a member of an elite coaching group. I do not ever imagine a time when I won't be. The support I get from my other Elite group members is extremely valuable. The fact that they are in business like me means they understand first hand what it's like. Your wife or partner may love you dearly but they are not qualified to offer you business advice. In fact, they will influence your business decisions based on their attitude to risk. If there is any hint that your livelihood could be at risk they will advise to take the safe route. The safe route is not always going to be the most lucrative. A coach or mentor will assess the situation with you and help you rationalise the opportunity, the risk and the reward. Then you will make an informed decision weighing up all the options.

Investing in a coach works on so many levels.

Chapter 5
MARKETING 101

Marketing Is Everything And Everything Is Marketing

Marketing for filmmakers can be very intimidating. I think it must have something to do with being creative; we seem to be more concerned with *creating content* than creating new business.

In simple terms, marketing is simply about putting your message in front of the right customers at the right time, so that when they are ready to make a buying decision, they think of you and call.

Marketing is just storytelling. People buy from people and therefore, if you wish to buy from someone, then it makes sense to have a relationship with them. Well executed marketing does just that. *It helps you build a relationship with the pontential customer, through different means of communicating.*

I like to compare marketing with fishing. You're looking to capture a specific type of customer and therefore you want to be looking in the places that they might be.

Think about it for a second. If you go fishing for salmon, you choose the right river. You choose the correct fishing rod, you choose the correct bait, and you choose the time of year when the salmon are most likely to be there. There would be no point trying to fish for salmon in a pond full of goldfish. Now, I am not a fisherman, but I imagine that the kind of bait used to catch salmon is not the same kind of bait you would use to catch goldfish.

If you take that principle and apply it to your marketplace, what do you get? Sales!

If you are in a business that sells wedding films, then who is it that makes the decision to hire you? I'm pretty certain it's the bride.

Therefore, where is the bride likely to be looking when considering her wedding? Notice I said *her* wedding! If you're reading this and you are married, you know exactly what I'm talking about. A wedding day is *all about the bride*. In fact, when I used to shoot weddings, I used to joke with the groom that he was the only person in the room who didn't get an official invitation. So, in terms of your marketing, the bride and the bride's mother are likely to be the *key influencers in making decisions about who to hire*.

If you are running a wedding film business, it's the bride and the bride's mother who you need to be connecting with. So where are they likely to be looking when planning a wedding? Well any number of places, but more likely they'll be looking at wedding magazines, going to wedding fayres and probably asking friends who are already married. (Hint: this is likely to be one of your biggest sources of business: recommendations and referrals.)

I've chosen weddings here as an example because it's a particularly competitive market. If you were to Google *'wedding video productions'* in your area, it's likely there will be quite a number of sites. This gives you some indication that other competing businesses are already doing some form of marketing online. Now, before becoming anxious that there is a lot of competition, this is a good thing. Lots of competition means there's likely to be lots of business, and the only decision you need to make is where are you going to pitch your business and price point.

I've had many videographers comment on how hard it is to make money in the wedding sector, and yet I have a couple of friends in the US who routinely charge in excess of $10,000 for a wedding. How? Well, they are *exceptional* at what they do and offer an exceptional service. Their films are unique, beautiful and epic and are priced accordingly. Don't forget, a wedding can be a great opportunity for the bride to brag about having the most expensive wedding filmmaker, as this can give her great kudos in some circles.

Human beings rarely make decisions on *need*, it's much more likely that they make decisions on *wants*. By that I mean they make decisions based on *an emotional reaction* (want) rather than a more logical need.

This is a *critical concept* to understand when marketing. A bride, for example, who is planning a wedding, has many things to consider; it's possible that the wedding video is way down the list of priorities. I'm almost certain that for the groom, it's an almost non-essential part of the wedding, and that is mostly because he knows it's likely to cost a lot of money. However if the bride decides she wants the wedding filmed, the groom is more than likely going to agree, because the last thing he wants on his wedding day is an unhappy bride.

So what does this have to do with marketing? Well, everything actually, because if you can build a relationship with the bride in advance of her wedding, and she decides that your service is exactly what she wants, then the price almost becomes irrelevant.

If you run a wedding film business and you're not marketing in some form or other, then you are leaving a considerable amount of money on the table.

For example; if you run a wedding film company that specialises in beautifully handcrafted reportage style wedding films, how do you communicate that with your potential audience?

Perhaps you already run some adverts; perhaps you do some advertising in local newspapers or magazines. But to become truly successful you have to be marketing on multiple levels simultaneously. The most dangerous number in business is **one;** one client, one supplier, one computer, one camera, one form of marketing.

Having multiple methods of attracting customers is a far more lucrative and sensible approach.

Google is one of the largest businesses and advertisers in the world. You wouldn't imagine they would have to do much to maintain the market position, would you? Yet they still send out direct response mail, they call you up, and they advertise. So if one of the biggest, most wealthy businesses in the world still markets to their potential customers, then so should you.

Here are 12 possible ways to attract customers:

- PR
- Referrals
- Advertising
- Email marketing
- Pay per click
- Joint ventures
- Trade shows and events
- Direct mail
- Internet advertising
- Direct sales
- Telemarketing

Consider each one of these as a pillar holding up the Greek Parthenon. If all 12 are functioning to some degree, then you're going to have a very stable Parthenon. If you try and hold up the roof of the Parthenon with only one or two of these pillars, it's likely the structure would not be so strong. Now, I cannot predict one way or the other which one of these will be the most successful

way to attract traffic, but the only way to discover if something is going to work for you, is to *test your approach.*

The most important thing to remember in marketing is this:
"Don't think! Test."

Different forms of marketing work better in different markets to different people. It's impossible to predict from a standing start which will work for you, so when you begin a marketing strategy you have to be open to the fact that some things will not work. The harsh fact of marketing is; if you don't test you will never know.

One thing is guaranteed; *if you do nothing*, you will achieve nothing and it's likely your business will not succeed.

Even if you pick only two or three approaches to begin with, at least you will be doing something to attract new business. The good news is there are actually many ways of automating a lot of these processes. Remember, at the beginning of this book I said that a lot of this is very simple, and it is (when you know how), but I also said it's not easy, because it involves a lot of effort.

Once you set some of these processes up, they can run on autopilot
and that is the genius of modern marketing.

But before we get into the details, let me explain the basics...

Solve the problem

Why do you use the internet? The reason search engines are called this is because generally, the person using them, is searching to solve a problem. It's as simple as that. Yes, occasionally, you may browse for browsing sake, but I would argue that the main reason why any of us type in a question is because we're looking to solve a problem. If you can really identify with this and apply it to your business, you're well on the way to growing a successful one.

When a client wants a video produced, the chances are they are doing it because they want to communicate a message to their customers, their clients or their stakeholders. The client is unlikely to care about what camera equipment you use and what problems you have in running your business. The client only cares about solving *their problem* and a savvy video producer will *identify this early on*, and *solve that problem for the client* with the minimal amount of fuss, which in turn will make the client's life easier.

More often than not, the client doesn't fully understand the extent of the problem they have. I had a client a few years ago who worked in a business that created security marking for computers and valuable items. They manufactured a very clever DNA spray that could mark property and give it a unique identification. They mostly sold to police forces and large corporations across Europe and the world. They had a large dealer network, which sold this for them. The major problem they had was that it was very difficult to fully appreciate what they produced and how it helped to protect valuables. So when the client approached me and said, *"how much to make a video?"* I then spent 45 minutes on the phone understanding more about what the product did and who their target customer was.

They had become very fixated with the fact that this product was created in a lab and had similarities to how DNA matching was used in the TV series CSI. The client kept referring to how they wanted a *'CSI style video'* to help sell it to the dealers. However, it became clear to me that this approach would be far too one-dimensional, and actually, what the client needed was some media that could be used by marketing agencies, which would help promote the application of this product to websites and news sites. They also had many enquiries from TV stations to do special stories on the product. However, even though the TV stations were really interested, they didn't have the budget to send a crew to cover each story individually. So I suggested creating what's called an electronic press kit (EPK). This would involve producing an interview with a leading spokesperson and a variety of B-roll that could be used by TV stations or news sites to create their own programmes. In addition, we would create and edit footage that would explain the process and the application of the synthetic DNA.

By spending time with the client - learning about the true nature of the problem they were trying to solve - we became a consultative partner that happened to be a video production company as well. Not only were we able to produce something for them that *solved the problem of communicating to the dealer network what it was the product did,* we also created footage which ended up being used in a national primetime BBC TV programme. National TV coverage like this would usually cost tens of thousands of dollars (if it were to be paid for in advertising screen time). But in this instance, it cost the client nothing other than the original cost of producing the content and editing. This particular example proved to be an incredible return on investment for that company. (On a side note, they have since come back to me twice to produce further content.)

If we apply the same concept to the wedding film example, you might argue, *"what is the problem you're trying to solve for the bride?"* Well that's simple, because most brides that I've met have admitted that they haven't got a clue about what makes a good video and what doesn't. It's often something they leave right to the last minute, because someone casually mentions, *"hey, you should get a video because after all you're spending all this money on the venue, flowers, the beautiful dress, and you've got those relatives flying over from Australia".* It's usually at *this point* that they start scurrying around trying to find someone. Personally, this is not a situation I would want to be in as a supplier, because you're left to the last minute and chances are there's not much left in the budget.

However, if you run a company with a solid marketing plan, then you're going to be getting in touch with this type of bride *months and months before the big day,* and by helping her appreciate the importance of having a beautifully handcrafted wedding film, she can then make the necessary plans to have one. Don't forget, you are competing with florists, venues, caterers, car hire, wedding dress makers, and a whole host of other businesses who want their slice of the wedding budget. If you can connect with the bride early on in the planning process, and you can help her understand and appreciate the true value of a beautiful film, then you're going to get a slice of that budget. Remember, once the wedding day is over and the food has been eaten and the alcohol has been drunk, what are they left with other than memories? This is where you can provide great value, because a beautiful film can be watched and remembered forever. Like I said earlier, you're solving a problem she doesn't know she has yet, and if you do this well, she will appreciate you and the work you've done for many years to come. More importantly, she will tell her friends about how wonderful your film was.

So, how do you begin a relationship with someone you've never met? Well, first you have to find them and I will be talking about this as we go through this chapter and the next. But once you've met that client - albeit virtually - you then need to *nurture the relationship* and the most effective way to do this is via email.

The Importance of Relationship Building

Email marketing done correctly is one of the single most effective ways of *building relationships* with prospects and clients. However, I also see lots of instances where email marketing is used in the wrong way too. Spamming (unsolicited email marketing), is most definitely the wrong way!

What I'm talking about is communicating with an audience who has given their *explicit permission for you to email them.* It is also imperative that the emails you send are highly relevant to that prospect, and this is based on what it was they signed up for in the first instance.

For example, on fstopacademy.com there is an opportunity for someone to 'opt in' on the homepage (and on every single page on the website). By 'opting in' they will then receive something in return. In this case, it's three *'free reports'*. Report one is the seven steps to creating cinematic images. Report two is how to avoid the five common mistakes when buying gear. And report three is the harsh truth about surviving in a video production business. Now, each of these reports has between four and six pages of useful information to help an aspiring filmmaker navigate through those three key areas. These reports have been written by me and are designed to offer *valuable advice* to a new filmmaker.

It is highly likely that if you're reading this book, then you've been to F-Stop Academy's website and possibly downloaded these reports. If you're on our email list, then it's almost certain that this is the case. These reports are called a *'lead generator'*. They are used to *'generate leads'* by giving you free advice in return for your first name and email address. Once you've submitted your details, you receive an email confirming that it's okay for us to send you those free reports as well as free filmmaking tips and emails. Once you confirm this (opt in), we then begin a relationship with you. I do this by sending 26 different emails over a two month period. Each of those emails is designed to build the relationship and give you an opportunity to decide if I am the right person to help you achieve your filmmaking goals.

You will also notice that at the bottom of each email there is an opportunity to unsubscribe (opt out), allowing you the choice to stop the emails at any time. This step is to make sure that the emails you receive *are* relevant and of benefit to you. This is a very important point to remember in email marketing. I welcome unsubscribes, and, in fact, I encourage it because I only want people on my email list who genuinely want to hear from me. If after 26 emails they decide it's no longer for them then that's fine - I don't want them on my list – in fact, occasionally, I send out an email to specifically clean out the list. I only want people who are potentially going to become buyers.

Once we've built a relationship (approximately two months) we then begin to make items available for sale, because at this point I'm confident that you will be in a position to make a decision about whether or not I am someone who can offer value to you.

What I am doing is simply trading free information in return for a relationship. It's often said that creating marketing and business relations are very similar to creating relations of a romantic nature.

It is only when we have built a significant relationship with you, will I start making products available for purchase. I want to gain your trust and for you to be happy with me, knowing that I will offer you value going forwards. You don't go proposing to someone you've just met in a bar, do you?

Remember, the reason you run a business is to make a profit. But trying to sell off the page in the first meeting is a no-go. The same is true when producing video for clients; you have to build a relationship before you start making sales.

Even if the client rings you up ad hoc and asks you to produce a product, the chances are they have called many other companies as well and are just looking for a price. In that instance you can still build a relationship (by asking questions), and that's exactly what I did with the client I mentioned previously. It might be worth adding that he was an aspiring filmmaker who had signed up for my reports and was actually on my email list. As a result of me emailing frequently when he needed some video production, he dropped me a line. He did this despite having an existing supplier, because we had built a relationship. And furthermore, when I produced a quote for him, he went a bit quiet. When I rang him up to discuss it, he said, *"we have had two other quotes,"* to which I replied, *"I'm guessing we were at least twice as expensive?"* His reply was *"yes"*. When I enquired as to why he got me to give him a quote he explained how he wasn't very happy with the existing company and that the third quote was from the niece of a board member who'd just finished film school. This then became a very simple conversation because a) he approached me and asked me to provide something that he wasn't getting from his existing supplier and b) the student option was not a competing option because it was just about doing it cheaply. (And if money was the issue, then this was the option to go for.) But I then reminded him of the value we'd gone through in discussing what would be the most appropriate film for them to make, and the true value of it being shown on television. Within 10 minutes he called me back and offered us the gig.

Let me repeat that, we were *twice as expensive* as the next best quotation, and yet we won the gig.

That is simply because we had *built a relationship*. I was providing incredible value and I'd presented the client with a scenario of what might go wrong should he use a cheaper option.

We are far more driven to go away from fear, as we are from attracting pleasure. If you put some doubt in a client's mind about using the cheaper option, and all the things that could potentially go wrong, then they are able to make a much more informed decision. Especially if you have explained that although you are more expensive, your expertise and know how will take away any potential risk and they will get a better product. Good people are never cheap and I'll talk more about this in the chapter about selling.

Email marketing played a huge part in this customer calling us up and asking us to shoot a project, because at the time I did not have a website that in any way offered this service. In fact, I'm fairly convinced that I could largely run fstopacademy.com without a traditional website and only use single 'landing page' websites - which I will explain about later.

Email marketing is part of something called *'direct response marketing'* and simply involves communicating directly with a subscriber who is giving you explicit permission to do so. Unfortunately, email marketing has been given a bad reputation because of a few unscrupulous marketing agencies. *However, used correctly, it is an extremely powerful sales tool.*

I have built F-Stop Academy's online business predominantly through email marketing. What's more, the emails that I send to my subscribers are personal and written like a friend writing to another friend. Most companies using email marketing get it very wrong. They make the emails HTML and full of graphics. I'm sure if you looked in your inbox right now there would be more than one of those style of emails, and the first thing those emails ask you to do is *'display images'* because they don't display normally.

Those type of emails are generic and very common in the corporate world. I do not suggest you use those kinds of emails, but rather personalise them in plain text. This is how I email my subscribers.

Another great advantage of email marketing is just how many people you can reach simultaneously around the globe. Using specially designed software you can write one email and send it out to your subscribers quickly and inexpensively. I'll be explaining more about exactly how to do this in the next chapter.

If you are not currently emailing your prospective customers then I strongly urge you to start. You may find some resistance to begin with, and that resistance will most likely come from within yourself. If you have not done this before then you need to make sure you do it correctly, and I will show you *exactly how to do this* in the next chapter.

Why Your Website Needs A Makeover

I mentioned in the previous section how I'd attracted work directly as a result of emailing prospects, and that work turned into a production job despite not having a production website. Why was that? Because I had *a relationship with the prospect*, one I had built up simply by sending them relevant and valuable content emails.

The biggest mistake I see when reviewing clients websites is that they all look the same. They generally have some fancy logo and a big video on the homepage displaying their latest show reel. The problem with this style of website is it's all about them and nothing to do with the customer they're trying to attract (or the problem that needs to be solved). They only care about solving their problem, and if the website is all about design, and not about solving the problem, then the chances are they will click away quickly.

There is a frightening statistic that you should be aware of: most people who visit a website, if they do not find what they're looking for *within seven seconds*, they click away and never return. So it doesn't matter how great the show reel might be, how talented you are, and how amazing you might be as a supplier, if they don't hang around long enough to discover more about you, then you've lost them forever.

The other big mistake websites make is they try to do too much on one page. I've been guilty of cramming lots of fancy design and functionality into a homepage in the past. There will be many discussions within the web design community that argue the need for lots of choice and options when landing on a homepage, but that is a fundamental mistake. The easiest way for someone to stay on your homepage is to offer them something for free in return for their email address. That way at least if they've visited and remained on the site long enough to claim something, you then have an opportunity the take that relationship further by using follow-up emails. To experience what this is like in practice, and if you haven't already done so, please visit www.fstopacademy.com and fill out your details in the 'opt in' box on the homepage, then see what happens.

I am continually *testing* my website to make it more effective with the simple goal of increasing the amount of people who opt in via my free report box. My web designer and my hosting company are always talking about amounts of traffic, but the only thing I am interested in is the *number of people who subscribe*. Once someone has subscribed and I have an email address, I can begin a relationship. Now, of course, not everyone who lands on the page subscribes, nor does everyone who subscribes end up becoming a customer, but I have a far larger chance of converting a visitor to a customer because I've nurtured them with an email sequence.

Most website designers do not understand *direct response marketing* and are far more focused on things looking pretty and having multi-functionality. It's very important to remember that when you hire a website designer, make sure they build something *you want* and not something they want; most likely fancy design and flashy fonts!

As I mentioned before, I'm continually testing my homepage at fstopacademy.com and I'm now at a point where I have stripped much of the original design down, so that there is a single, clear purpose. I still have some navigation options because it's helpful for Google, particularly when advertising, but the main purpose of the homepage is to get someone to sign up to my email list. I strongly suggest you do the same. (By the time this book is published, I may be testing out different homepage layouts, it's an ongoing process.) Now, you may find yourself resistant to this approach because it will likely take you out of your comfort zone, but trust me if you begin to email your customers (with valuable and relevant material), your business will increase. I once sold $65,000 worth of online courses in a week, simply as a result of sending emails.

Email marketing works and you should be designing your website so that this becomes a key strategy in your own business. I will repeat again, email marketing works if done correctly, and I have yet to find a business where it can't be effective.

Another bad habit of website designers is when they suggest having lots of external links to things like YouTube, Vimeo and other social media sites. This is just plain crazy, because if you get someone visiting your website why on earth would you want them to click away and start watching YouTube videos or go to your social media links? When a new visitor lands on your website the purpose should be simple; *capture their details so you can begin a relationship with them.* The rest you can follow up at a later date. Remember, a visitor is scouring the internet to *find a solution to a problem.* If you can help them solve it, your business will grow.

So, whether you're designing your first website or are looking to update your existing one, focus on capturing your visitors' details and solving a problem, otherwise they will just click away and they are lost for good.

Don't waste time on social media

Social media is the new shiny thing that many would have you believe is *key* to their success. In my experience, Twitter and Facebook have been responsible for a *tiny amount of business*. In order for Twitter to be effective you have to be tweeting constantly, and while there may be some value, the amount of effort required versus the return is usually not worthwhile. Certainly not as effective and not as measurable as capturing email addresses and communicating via email (which can be automated and doesn't require a lot of time to execute once the initial process has been set up).

Now there may be exceptions to the rule, but I've yet to hear a compelling story from a business that has had great success with Twitter or Facebook.

Advertising on Facebook can be extremely effective, but beware; simply getting *'likes'* to your business page is largely a waste of time. (I'm going to go into the effectiveness of Facebook, Google and YouTube advertising in the next chapter.) The main reason social media is ineffective for business reasons, is it tends to be an *outward only* conversation. I must emphasise that there may be situations where filmmakers have had positive experiences, but I will still maintain that overall the amount of time and resources taken to generate business from social media outweighs the return. I'm not saying don't do it at all, but be measured in how much time and effort you put into it.

At the time of writing, I have 6611 followers on Twitter and 5356 likes on the F-Stop Academy Facebook page. The trouble is I have no way of identifying *if any of those Twitter followers or Facebook likes actually become customers.* And if you can't measure it, you can't decide if it's effective or not. Now I do very little to promote what we do on Facebook and Twitter. In fact, I'm more likely to post a picture of my dog than something to do with filmmaking. Interestingly, the pictures that get the most likes and the most engagement are the ones of gear. The trouble with Facebook likes is that there is no commitment from the person liking the image. I can post an event on my Facebook page which has got over 5300 likes, but it's likely most of them won't turn up, so really, what's the point? So be very wary of investing too much time driving people to a fan page and focus instead on winning new business through capturing data and following up via email.

However, there are exceptions; my wife runs a reflexology business and she has been noticing a large amount of referral business coming via Facebook. My analysis of this has concluded that women spend up to 10 times more time on Facebook and community environments recommending products and services to each other. This can have a great impact, which can be seen in her business. (She has seen growth in posting daily on her Facebook page.) So, never say never, but if I were to recommend the best use of your time and resources, prioritise email opt in and develop a website that focuses on getting your visitors' contact details. Once you have these and you begin a relationship with them, it's from there you can suggest liking your Facebook page and adding them as a follower on various social media streams.

Become An Expert In Your Niche

I talked earlier about the production we carried out for the security company. When the client approached me, he had been an email subscriber for some time and he'd read enough to decide that I was an expert. He had already used a production company on previous jobs, but clearly wasn't happy with the outcome. He then paid twice as much to use me instead of them.

When you become an expert and gain the trust of customers, they will *pay more* for your expertise. This is because they perceive your expertise as a bringing more value to their production.

When I say, *"I am the world's leading authority on business training for filmmakers,"* you might question that claim. It is true and I can back it up if anyone challenges me on that. In 2013, I gave a talk at the broadcast video expo in London. It was entitled *'How to avoid becoming one of the 95% of struggling filmmakers,'* and the talk was all about the business of filmmaking. There was standing room only at the event - I would guess in excess of 200 people - and the broadcast video expo organisers have already asked me to give the same talk at next year's event. Being able to talk at events like these really increases my credibilty of being an 'expert'. But the most significant action I have taken in backing up that statement is that I have written a book on the subject. I am an author of a book called *'Business For Filmmakers'* and that positions me above everyone else that might be doing this kind of education. The truth is, I have not come across anyone else who's offering the full level of business education as I am. I am a leading expert on this topic. Sometimes, it's enough just to make the claim. I, however, regard my integrity with great importance and therefore back that up with the book and the various business resources that are attached to the subject. I also have a track record of helping business owners in the production industry grow their business to six figures and beyond. I run a monthly *'business for film makers Inner circle'* and an ongoing annual coaching program (details at the end of the book). I have countless cases studies of successful filmmakers who have applied my principles.

In another example, I was talking to one of my elite coaching clients about his business. He runs a production company in Denmark and specialises in creating testimonial films for corporate clients. We were discussing ways in which he could expand his business and increase his rates to attract better customers. I suggested that he become *'Denmark's leading authority'* on the creation of customer testimonial videos and position everything on his website to back that up. It worked brilliantly!

To prove this point further, let me tell you what I was willing to pay to fix a problem I was having. I injured my leg in 2001 and I developed arthritis of the right ankle. I did some research and decided, on the advice of my physiotherapist, to have the pins and plate removed which had been fitted at the time of the accident. In addition to this, I had also been advised that by using keyhole surgery, a surgeon could clean up the joint and alleviate some of the pain I was experiencing. I had two choices: wait six months just to get an appointment on the National Health Service or pay for a private consultation with one of the UK's leading experts and authorities on ankle injuries. I chose the latter. From memory, I paid about £3000 to have my ankle operated on. I didn't question the cost because I was dealing with one of the *leading experts* and I did not want to compromise by using a general practitioner. 10 years on from that operation, I don't suffer nearly the pain I used to.

If you become the leading authority in your particular market niche, then when you present that offering to the marketplace you will attract more business.

The fact is, when we need to engage someone professionally to help us solve a problem, we want the best supplier that we can afford. If we are given the option of three suppliers and one is an expert in that field, whilst the other two are generalists, we are far more likely to choose the specialist.

Now, the really clever thing about positioning yourself as an expert in your field is that nobody expects expertise to be cheap. By becoming the expert, your prices become elastic. It's the same reason I was able to charge twice the price of the nearest competitor when I produced the security marking video.

The same is true in video production. There are plenty of general practitioners in the video production business, but if you become a specialist, or choose a niche and become an expert within that niche, you can potentially charge what you want.

Get testimonials

I mentioned earlier that my wife has been having great success with referrals. Referrals and testimonials are some of the most *powerful means of marketing,* especially in the creative industries. We love recommendations from others who share our interest in a common subject. In my own business of running filmmaking workshops, I'll often ask attendees what it was that helped them make a decision to attend. In almost every case, it's the testimonial videos on the sales pages for the workshops.

When making any buying decision, we are always fighting in our minds about spending the money and what we can get in return. But when we are faced with other people sharing their delight in attending an event, it is very compelling viewing and usually helps make the final decision.

Importantly, I record these testimonial videos on a Sony NX 30 or my iPhone. You might think this is a simplistic approach but the reason I do this is because it produces a more *authentic feel*. If a testimonial looks too produced, it loses some of the realism. I always ask attendees to record testimonial videos right at the end of a class and I do it while there is still chattering going on in the room. I also try to avoid any editing, because what I want is a real response at the point when they've just finished the class. It's one of the *single most important aspects* in my business for attracting new customers.

My events are not cheap; the average price is $1000 for two days so I'm only interested in attracting people who see the true value in attending a small group workshop.

If you look at the first few pages of this book, it's filled with testimonials; so when someone picks it up in a bookstore, they are presented with accolades and positive feedback about the value of my training. This might well be reason enough for them to buy the book.

So, if you've done work for a client and they have had a great result, ask them for a testimonial. It doesn't have to be filmed, it could just be written. Although, in some instances, written testimonials can be perceived as fake, so when you can, get and use the full name of the person who has written it, as this can help give the testimonial credibilty. In fact, LinkedIn has a great function where you can ask for someone to endorse you and these can be very powerful. It's one thing to tell the world that you're a great filmmaker and offer a great service, it's far more powerful for someone else to say this for you.

As we bring this chapter to a close, I just want you to think about everything that's been discussed. Some of this may be new to you and some of it may be familiar. Hopefully, I've covered the basics, and in the next chapter I want to go into more specific strategies of how to achieve a constant stream of new clients.

Chapter 6

AUTOMATE YOUR MARKETING SYSTEM

Part 1; How To Create Your Lead Generator

As I discussed in the previous chapter, building a relationship with your potential customer is vitally important, as this gains trust and allows you to then present a buying option.

I've also spoken about our free report that we offer to visitors, and this next chapter is all about how to create that report and how to set up your emails so that they are automated. When you know how, it's super easy!

Create some valuable free content and give it away for free

When someone is searching the internet looking to solve a problem, there is nothing more powerful than landing on a page which not only promises to solve the problem, but actually gives them a free gift which helps them solve it more quickly. This is sometimes known as 'free line content' or 'lead generator' and it's designed to lure your prospect into signing up (or 'opting in') to receive more information from you.

The psychology behind this process is designed to create a good impression with a prospective customer. It also puts you in control early on in the buying cycle.

Let me explain: if your ideal client is browsing the internet looking to find a corporate video production company to create a promotional video, and they are using the search term *'corporate video production'*, they'll no doubt have many companies (results) to choose from. Let's say they then click on two or three different companies. The chances are they will all offer a similar kind of service, including headlines like, *'look at our showreel'*, *'click here for a quote...'* and so on.

Now imagine if one of those results offers them a free report called, *'Five tips to help you choose a video production company and how to avoid making an expensive mistake!'* I bet they would be intrigued. There is the answer to their problem, and they don't have to wade through lots of other websites, as they now have a company which offers them a free report that will help them make their decision. (A very important psychological trick here is to include the phrase *"avoid making an expensive mistake"*. It's quite possible that the person tasked with finding a production company has budgetary restraints or at the very least a figure in mind that they want to spend.) So it's your job as a marketer to highlight the pain and then offer an easy solution to help put their mind at ease, especially if you run a professional high quality business that charges premium prices.

A second benefit of creating a free report like this is that not many people go to the trouble of doing this, which means you instantly stand out from the rest of the noise. Go now and Google *'corporate video production'* and browse the companies which are advertising. My guess is that *very few, if any*, are offering this kind of free report on their homepage.

This is the biggest and easiest no-brainer that you can apply to your business immediately.

How to create your report

Creating a report like this is very easy. You can simply write down the five most commonly asked questions you get from clients when they make their initial enquiry. You can then break down this further by giving each of those questions three subheadings and answer those questions in detail. You will then end up with 15 points of valuable information that will help the client make an informed choice. All you have to do next is fill in the blanks and have a designer format it into a professional looking PDF document. Then simply upload this to your website and make it available for download, but only once someone has 'opted in' (given you their email address and name) in return for the report.

It doesn't even have to be a PDF report. It could be a podcast, free video series, or even a book. The most important thing is that it is perceived as having value and goes some way to solving their problem.

It's very important not to offer anything for sale in this first communication. The psychological purpose of a *'free gift'* is that it offers the client great value and you will have embedded in their mind that you are someone who is willing to help them before any money has exchanged hands. *This is a very strong and powerful marketing tool.*

When someone gives you anything, be it a bottle of wine for dinner or a thank you gift of any description, you feel a great sense of warmth and joy because it is nice to receive presents. If someone buys you lunch, you often have it in your mind that you *'owe'* them a lunch in return. If someone has done a favour for you or helped you out in some way, you are naturally drawn to wanting to help them in return. By creating a free report that helps someone solve a problem (and if they find it helpful) then it's quite likely you will feature highly on their list of people to contact to carry out the actual work.

> *This is simply human psychology; when you give something away for free, you endear yourself to that person, just by being helpful.*

In my own business www.fstopacademy.com, we offer free reports to get you started and then we follow up with email. Only after a two-month period do we begin to offer products for sale. Nobody likes the hard sell without a bit of understanding in advance of who you're dealing with, and what knowledge and experience you have to offer.

Once you've created a report and it's on your website, what happens next? Well, now you have to create a series of emails and an *'opt in'* form so that you can capture the data (contact details) and follow up with that customer regularly via email.

Part 2; How To Set Up Your Automated Email Responder

So, you may be asking, what exactly is an email auto responder?

In simple terms, an email auto responder is a piece of software that allows you to automatically send emails to multiple subscribers at the same time.

Your group of subscribers is often known as your *'list'*, and in some cases, these lists can grow to many thousands of people.

The beauty of this style of marketing is that it's very efficient because you can send one email to 10,000 people with the click of a mouse.

There are numerous companies offering this service.

Popular email auto responders include:

- Aweber
- Mailchimp
- Constant Contact
- Get Response
- Infusion Soft
- Ontraport

You can find links to all of these suppliers at www.businessforfilmmakers.com/resources

There are two key aspects to working with auto responders. The first part is called an *'opt in' form*. This is the little box which asks for your name and email address, and you need to add this to your web page.

This webpage is often known as a landing page and will typically have a headline, a sub headline and a call to action (CTA). The headline is designed to grab the attention of the web visitor, and the sub headline generally offers the information that person might be looking for.

The call to action is simply instructions telling the person that if they want the information (free report) they just need to fill in their name and email address in the box and the report will be sent to them immediately.

The second key element is the emails themselves. Once the person has done this, the auto responder goes to work. Firstly the auto responder will send an email confirming that they want to receive the information they've just requested. This is known as a *'double opt in'* process and it's very important that you get this second permission before sending them the report and further emails. (By getting this secondary confirmation, it means that this person is absolutely sure they want to receive your emails, and that they didn't just 'accidentally' gave you their name and email address.)

Once this step has been completed, the auto responder will then automatically send the report and all subsequent follow up emails! Magic!

There is some work involved in setting up the auto responder sequence explained above, plus you now need to write a number of emails which will be sent at regular intervals once the report has been sent. But once you've done it, every time a new subscriber fills out their details on your landing page, the auto responder kicks in and will send out these emails automatically. This means that while you are filming jobs or on holiday, this system communicates with that prospective customer with no additional work from you.

I have no idea why more businesses do not use this method, because it's simple, cheap and a very effective way of nurturing customers, and all of it's done automatically.

These emails then nurture the relationship, leading to, and maybe offering the prospect a chance to give you a call or better still, you contact them at an appropriate time to discuss their project and how you might be able to help them. The advantage of this method of *lead nurture* is that you get an opportunity to show your personality to the prospect before the point at which you need to get on the phone.

Of course, there is no reason why at the end of every email, you have an offer for them to give you a call. For example, you could have a P.S. that says, *"if you're ready to discuss a project, please call and see how I can help you further"* and insert your phone number. Identifying what works best for your market is something that you can only develop over time and don't forget to test.

With software like Infusion Soft (which is what I use), it's possible to create very advanced sequences that trigger other sequences depending on the activity of the person reading an email and them clicking a link that is embedded into that message.

However, to keep things simple at the beginning – especially if this is all new to you - just emailing regularly is the secret to building a relationship. The frequency of contact keeps you in the mind of the person reading the email so that when they are ready to make a buying decision, you are in their subconscious.

Now, if you're worried that you're emailing too much, don't panic. Not every email you write will be read. But the simple process of your name popping up into their inbox on a regular basis will cause something very significant to happen. Basically, when that prospect needs the solution to what you have to offer, who are they going to turn to? Most likely, the person that has been sending them informative email, on a regular basis, and the author of the free report that helped them with their initial issue.

So, remember, if you make it easy for that person to choose you, you immediately separate yourself from all of the other companies they may have been considering, simply by putting yourself in front of them on a regular basis.

Now one final point that is vital to remember; *you can't just send any old email whenever you like,* it has to be relevant to the page the prospect first landed on.

Only send relevant information that directly relates to the initial enquiry. That way you have a greater chance of succeeding in winning the business.

So, this is how you set up your autoresponder sequence, now let's look at further ways of getting *targeted prospects* onto your website.

Chapter 7
HOW TO ATTRACT CUSTOMERS

Forget About SEO, Advertise On Facebook And Google

It's a popular myth that if you design your website with the correct keywords and optimise your page for search engine optimisation, you will get onto the first page of Google.

The trouble is, Google are continually changing the algorithms that dictate what aspects of a page is most relevant and therefore the websites that then get displayed. Google is an advertiser and its number one priority is to attract advertisers to pay for the service. This is why in recent years, the emphasis on SEO has been diminishing in favour of *paid advertising*. I know many businesses which have had great success with Google's *'pay per click'* advertising.

Pay per click (PPC) works very simply. You create an advert using keywords or phrases that someone may type in when searching on Google, and when Google thinks your advert is relevant to that search phrase, they will then display your advert to that person. The really clever part about PPC is that *you only pay* if someone clicks on your advert.

Many businesses use pay per click to advertise their business, but 80% of them make a fundamental mistake with this strategy. This mistake is caused when the prospect has to browse the site or hunt for the answer for which they clicked the advert to solve (or ultimately clicks away because the answer isn't obvious). This can become a very expensive way of advertising because if you are paying for each click and losing the customer as soon as they get to your website, then you're throwing money down the drain. A far more intelligent method is to advertise and drive people to your *landing page*, where the only option available to them is to fill out their details and download your free report. (Starting your auto responder sequence and beginning the relationship.)

Using this method of paid advertising - leading your prospect to a landing page and then engaging the follow up process - allows you to track the effectiveness of your advertising spend. By measuring and testing different aspects of your campaign, you can optimise it so that it works at its most efficient.

Once you have over 100 visitors signing up for your report, you can use analytics software (get it free from Google - www.google.com/analytics/) to track how effective your advertising is. It's not uncommon for less than one person out of every hundred to take any action, but by using the landing page approach with a free report, you can easily increase that to between five and 20 people out of every hundred who visit your website.

The real value of pay per click advertising with Google is the quality of leads you acquire through this method. If someone is actively searching for corporate video production then they are very motivated. If they then click on your advert and download your report, the chances are they are a very hot prospect. Compare that to someone who has just stumbled across your website (perhaps they've clicked a link on another person's site that's taken them to yours). It's much less likely they are as motivated as someone who is actively searching to solve a problem.

This style of advertising is not limited to Google. *Yahoo, Bing, Linkedin* and *Facebook* all offer similar types of advertising opportunities. (*YouTube* is owned by Google, and it also offers advertising like PPC.)

Facebook

Facebook advertising is quickly becoming the new gold rush of cheap marketing. What makes Facebook advertising so powerful is the amount of data that Facebook has about all of its members.

If you work in the wedding business, for example, then you need to be advertising on Facebook because the first thing a bride does when she gets engaged is change her status on Facebook, and it's quite likely she will begin posting all of the details of her impending nuptials. As an advertiser, you can directly target women who are getting married within a six-month, 12 month or 18 month time frame, and you can produce adverts exclusively to that market.

You could create a free report called, *"10 things every bride needs to know about choosing a wedding filmmaker and how to avoid the wedding video cowboys"*, and then run these on Facebook, targeting newly engaged women.

Customers who you've had to 'pay for' generally result in a higher quality prospects than relying on SEO or other free traffic sources. I'm not saying you don't want people opting in organically, but higher quality prospects tend to come from paid traffic. The other really interesting aspect of paid traffic is that once you test and measure, it's not uncommon to see a 300% or 400% return on investment. Once you get the system working it becomes a licence to print money because if you spend £10 on acquiring a customer and that customer spends £40 then you're making a £30 profit for every £10 spent.

Split Testing

Everything that I'm teaching you in this book is very simple, however, it's not always easy and it involves a great deal of effort. Unfortunately, it will also require a few failures along the way, but making mistakes and failing is a vitally important part of becoming a great marketer, because every time something doesn't work, you're getting closer to understanding *what does*.

The good news is that you can test each approach, and I'm going to introduce a term called *'split testing'*, which you can apply to your marketing efforts with the help of software.

For example: with Facebook advertising you can run multiple variations of an advert within the same campaign. The headline and the text can be identical, but you can change the image or photograph. Then, when you run the advert, Facebook will automatically auto rotate the advert using the different pictures. After a few days of testing, you can then review the results.

You will generally find that one advert will stand out as being much more successful than the other. You can then pause the adverts that are not performing very well, and 'split test' another variation of the *successful* advert. This could simply be a change of headline. You then run *those adverts* for a little longer until you see which one is performing best. This is known as *'A/B split testing'* and helps you optimise an advert until such time as it's performing as best it can, at which point you can *increase your spend* (or cost for that advert) with a repeatable and predictable return on investment.

There are a number of tools available to help with split testing. **Leadpages.net** offer A/B split testing within their templates. They also offer custom built landing pages that can be hosted on your server or embedded on your website. Within this software you can split test pages simultaneously and have software reports tell you how well one did over the other.

Other services like **optimizely.com** allow you to split test your website. Split testing takes the guesswork out of what's working and what isn't.

Another valuable tool is **crazyegg.com** This is heat map software that analyses where people look on your website and shows you what tabs and links they click, as well as where people are coming from.

Sometimes simply changing the colour of your text can increase response. We ran a test recently on our home page (fstopacademy.com) where we just changed the colour of the background in the 'opt in' box from red to yellow, and we saw a 5% increase.

Another test we performed was looking at which words were more popular. We tested *"free resources"*, *"free training"*, *"free tutorials"* and *"free videos"* over a six month period and discovered that *"free training"* was the most popular of those four variants.

Split testing is a very useful tool that can be applied across your online presence. It takes the emotion out of running your business because it *scientifically measures* what people do on your website, what they click and what actions they take.

The benefits of free PR

I talked earlier about the importance of being seen as an expert in your niche. Experts are always in demand, be it in magazines, podcasts and in guest blog articles. Whenever I am asked to contribute to a magazine article, I always say *yes* because the small amount of time it takes me to create the article exposes me to an audience that may not yet know who I am, what business I run or how I may be able to help.

Currently, I am writing a column for a professional filmmaking magazine that is going to be about *business for film makers*. It makes perfect sense for me, because every three months I have a five page article going out (and being read by) aspiring professional filmmakers. In return for contributing, I get to talk about my book and make the book available for sale within the covers of the magazine. This means a certain number of people who read the article will go on to buy my book and ultimately opt in to my auto responder sequence and follow up.

To buy the equivalent five full pages of advertising in a specialist magazine could cost in excess of £5000 per issue (multiply that by four, and you're looking at £20,000 per year). Instead, I get the same exposure *for fee* and get my views and teachings printed in the targeted magazine. (I could likely write 1,800 words in around 4 hours; if my time is valued at £200 per hour that is an £800 cost, returning £5,000 worth of PR. A solid ROI.)

If you become an expert in your niche then you could be offered the same opportunity. In an earlier chapter, I mentioned a client of mine based in Denmark who specialises in making customer testimonial videos. He was also able to do the same thing and it's been very beneficial for him.

Trade magazines have the same dilemma every month. Before an issue is even considered, there are a number of blank pages that need to be filled with relevant articles to satisfy the readership. Magazine editors are continually looking for good stories and contributors. If you are an expert and are willing to do the work, this is an incredible source of free publicity.

Trade Shows and Conventions

Another great source of free publicity is to offer your services to relevant trade shows and conventions. Let's go back to my wedding filmmaker example. I would guess that there are hundreds of bridal fairs and shows, which, if you were to contact the organiser, you could ask if they were planning to have any free seminars. If so, you could offer to fill a 30 to 45 minute session that would be relevant to brides attending the wedding fair.

In the same way that magazine editors are looking to fill pages of every issue, organisers of tradeshows and conventions are looking to fill speaking slots at seminars. This can be another way of amplifying your expert status. Combine that with writing articles for wedding magazines and you could position yourself head and shoulders above your competition.

This is not just limited to the wedding market; it works across all facets of video production. This is why I believe it is so important to become an expert and a specialist. A great friend and client of mine, David West, who is based in Australia, specialises in filming medical operations, which are then used to teach and educate other junior surgeons. My client makes a point of building very strong relationships with these surgeons and he spends a great deal of time with them, making him the 'go to' guy for a number of top surgeons who want their operations filming.

This is a perfect example of a specialist and because he is an expert, he isn't cheap. Westy flies all over Australia filming and working with top surgeons, as well as running a very successful business specialising in medical filmmaking. In fact, he told me recently that he has too much work - he cannot do it all.

You could do the same. Perhaps you could specialise in making films for estate agents and realtors. You could focus on the high value properties and work with a few top estate agents. You could write an article all about the value of a handcrafted film to help sell high-value property. If you become the person who is the expert in this particular area, and are able to get articles published on the subject, then this will elevate your position in the eyes of the reader.

Direct Mail

In the world of constant contact, social media and instant communication, there can be so much noise it can be very hard to get your message through to the decision maker. Which is why old fashioned direct mail sent in the post can be extremely effective at capturing the attention of a prospective client or customer.

Particularly with higher priced offerings, a letter sent in the mail is more likely to be read than a simple email. Partly because very few businesses do this anymore, but if you do it right, it can be very effective.

A couple of years ago, we ran a music video master class in London for only 12 students. The cost of the program was £2,500 per person for a four-day programme. While we marketed this via email and via a sales page on the website, I also sent out hand addressed and signed letters to 100 people. Importantly, we hand wrote the name and address on each letter, and used a stick on stamp. Out of the 12 students who attended, four responded to the handwritten letter. The net result of four hours' work (writing and addressing the letters) yielded £10,000 of sales. The other £20,000 of sales came as a result of email marketing. And these people were respondents of my free report and so had received my follow up emails.

Direct mail can take many forms, including:

- Postcards
- Tear sheets
- Newsletters
- Handwritten letters
- Free gifts

It's anything that is sent by traditional mail. I began testing a newsletter at the beginning of 2014. I only sent out one issue, and the response was incredible. Many of the comments I received were along lines of, *"wow, it was so nice to get something in the mail. I'd forgotten what it was like to receive something I could read that didn't involve a screen or a battery"*. (Unfortunately, I wasn't able to publish any more newsletters, as I became incredibly busy with other projects, but it's certainly something I will consider in the future.)

I have mentioned before that I am part of a mastermind group myself and we meet every three months in Ireland. This is made up of 14 different business owners, all working across different sectors. I know from speaking with my colleagues that many of them are sending out a monthly newsletter, not an e-newsletter, but an actual printed hardcopy newsletter that their customers receive in the mail. They all share similar stories of customers taking particular notice of the fact that they are doing something different, and everyone has seen an increase in business because of it.

If you remember in Chapter 4 (Marketing 101) I spoke about the marketing pillars and the marketing Parthenon. Direct mail is one of those pillars. Now, I'm not suggesting that you immediately go out and start spending money on printing and mailing printed newsletters, you need to choose which of these methods you believe will work most effectively for your market sector and test each approach, but it's something that is worth considering.

The single most important thing to remember in all aspects of marketing is to ignore what people think. And by people I mean your colleagues, your wife, your husband, your partner, your friends…The only people you should listen to are the customers who pay you money.

Everybody will have an opinion on how you are running your business, and if you begin this style of marketing you will be facing some resistance; possibly from people you even work with. This is because most people are uncomfortable with this style of direct response. You have to ignore them and only listen to your customers. People will vote with their wallets, and that is why you are in business. However, no matter what method you choose, remember… everything you do is a test, and this leads nicely on to…

Don't think, test!

Testing and measuring are the most important results that you need to focus on to grow your business. Like I mentioned above, everybody will have an opinion on how you are running your business, and you need to stay focused on the results.

Let your customers decide what is working.

Interestingly when I'm running a campaign to promote the launch of a new product, I generally increase the frequency and tone of my sales emails. This can result in unsubscribes (people opting out of my emails), but that's a good thing because if they have not bought anything after two or three months, then it's not likely that they are ever going to buy anything anyway. If they get offended because I'm making a fantastic product available to them, which I know will benefit them, then I don't want to deal with them as customers. It's a self-selecting process. For every negative email I get (telling me not to send them emails any more), I get an equal number of emails telling me how much they appreciate how I run my business and how I help. This is a very valuable lesson; you will never please everyone so don't even try. I'd much rather please the customers who love what I do, at the expense of people who are cynical and don't get it.

I actually don't care about the people who are not interested in what I offer, I only care about my customers.

You cannot please everyone, so don't try. Focus on being an expert in a niche that absolutely blows the competition away, and be the 'go to' person in your sector.

Now, hopefully you have started to see some increase in your customer numbers, and your autoresponder is now working a treat at engaging and building a relationship with them, so let's look at how to deal with them going forwards.

Chapter 8
DEALING WITH CLIENTS

Explaining The Cost vs Benefit

For many clients, the prospect of commissioning a video production leaves one key consideration in their minds and that is: *"how much is it all going to cost?"* Particularly for marketing departments or smaller businesses which may only spend a nominal amount of money on advertising. Video production by its very nature involves more personnel and more costs and will likely be inherently more expensive than some graphic design work or print advertising.

If you want to grow and build a successful video production business, you have to start thinking from the client's perspective. The client just sees video as a cost in the early stages. That's why so many clients are price driven. How many times have you had an email or a phone call in which price comes up in the first five minutes?

Video production is expensive and when you start hiring crew and factor in post-production and all the other associated costs, things can start to add up. So your role as a producer is to help the clients fully understand the benefits and reach of video, over other traditional forms of communication. You need to work with the client to help them understand that any spend should be viewed with a clear return on investment (ROI).

A visitor to a website is more likely to watch a one minute video than read a block of copy because watching a video is far less labour intensive than reading a block of text. And it's this key benenfit that you need to explain to clients who are expanding their advertising to video.

This goes beyond just shooting and editing a video; you have to help the client feel comfortable that while there may be a greater initial outlay than perhaps they are used to, the benefits of video can be far reaching.

Many clients may understand the necessity of reaching a far wider audience, but many will not understand the process involved in producing video to a high standard. Some may be attempting to create their own videos, the iPhone, for example, is a very capable video camera and there are many 'how to' videos on YouTube.

Your job is to persuade the client that by creating a high-quality video, it will give a far greater impression to their customer. And with a bit of pre-planning, you could shoot a lot of different content within one day of filming, and although this may come at a cost, it could be a real investment long term.

I'm currently working on a project that involves a celebrity being booked to endorse a product. The celebrity fee is significant and runs to tens of thousands of pounds. In order to take full advantage of the shooting day, we are planning to shoot between 10 and 15 different films. Those can then be edited and released throughout the year to spread the cost. So while the overall production may cost the client £60,000, when we create 15 short videos, and then spread them out over the year and incorporate them in different marketing activity, then each video has cost only £4000.

Particularly in corporate organisations, breaking down these larger figures into a cost per piece can sometimes ease the shock of a larger number. So the £4000 per video price can be streaming on their website, and be sent out to clients, and they can drive social media and other traffic to web pages.

You simply have to help your client understand the benefits of using video.

Remember, most businesses are very focused on the volume, by that I mean website visitors and website traffic. Many focus on the bigger numbers because more traffic equals more sales. One way to help the client understand the ROI of video, is to ask them to do some simple math.

For example; let's imagine Bob who manufactures custom alloy wheels. He currently sells 10 sets of alloy wheels per week and makes $5000 profit. Taking a four week month as an average, Bob is currently making $20,000 per month profit. Over the course of the year, that's $240,000.

Let's now imagine you could make a series of videos showing the craftsmanship, care and hand detailing on that product. That video could then be uploaded to YouTube and promoted. If he was able to sell an extra five sets of alloy wheels per month, he'd make an extra $2500 profit. That is an additional $30,000 in a year.

If you now asked Bob how much he was willing to spend in order to increase five more sets of sales per month that were worth $30,000 a year, he may be willing to spend one third of that extra profit. In truth, he may well be able to sell even more than those predicted five extra sales per month, but it's about educating the customer what is possible, and how a video could really be a fantastic return on investment. The really great aspect of this example is that – more than likely, Bob will make more sales than predicted - and with more sales, he's likely to ask for more videos. This method of approaching clients from their point of view (what's in it for them) is more likely to have greater outcomes for you and your video business

But, from your perspective, you could shoot that video in one day, and create either one five-minute film or five short example films. Would you be interested in charging $10,000 for a three day project?

Taking this simple example, if you did two projects like this per month, taking only six days of work, you could be generating over $200,000 per year in revenue.

Make your client's life easier

Your prospective clients have lots of hassle to deal with in their day-to-day business life, and video production can be a labour intensive process and generate an additional workload for them. I always like to think of myself as a friendly consultant when working with clients. *I want to make their life easy,* hold their hand through the process of producing video so they get the full benefit with the minimum amount of hassle. I like to operate in a professional but friendly manner; without compromising exclusivity or availability.

Demonstrating that you have the best interests of your client's goal in mind, in my experience, makes for smoother production. Much of the time confusion can arise because of mismanaged expectations. As video producers we have insight and experience in how long things can take, but clients who are new to video and the production process often don't realise how slow the process can be.

Clearly laying out in advance how long things take and preparing your client for likely delays helps everyone have a greater understanding of what to expect on a shoot day.

One of the reasons why I charge premium prices is simply so I can dedicate *all of my time* to a client project. I explain this to clients early on in the process. I make it clear that we're not the cheapest video producers and that the reason for that is because we don't take on multiple projects simultaneously. The benefit to the clients is that when they engage us, they have all of our resources at their disposal.

I recall several years ago, when Sam and I were having the house renovated, our builder began the project as well as three or four other jobs at the same time. As the months progressed we saw less and less of his team finishing our house. I found it incredibly frustrating and I lost all faith in the supplier, and ultimately we fired him.

It is very important in my view that you don't just look at clients as one offs, but rather look to build a lifelong relationship with them, so they will come back to you again and again. Depending on the size of the job and the value, this may not always be practical but I try very hard to maintain this position.

I find that taking on one project at a time allows me to focus my attention on making it the best it can be. However, the only way that works is by ensuring that it's financially lucrative enough to do so. People buy from people and I've yet to find an example of a client who doesn't value and appreciate my honesty, and is willing to pay the price to have that exclusivity.

Another key benefit of this approach is that you have more brain space to think ahead and pre-empt problems that the project might experience. You will then be able to apply solutions before it becomes a problem to the client. It's all about giving the client the best possible experience you can, and really helping them reduce their level of stress when something like this is needed to be produced.

Be accountable

Things can and do go wrong on productions; it can be down to the location, the talent, technical issues and all sorts of other *'out of your control problems'*, but one thing is for sure, you need to take responsibility and be accountable to the smooth running of the production. As a producer it's your job to ensure it runs smoothly, which includes having backup plans and always thinking about the *'what if'* scenario.

Having a professional but friendly communication, which is open and direct and maintains accountability, will go a long way in smoothing over any problems. This might be intimidating if you've not done much producing before, but somebody has to be in charge of the process and ultimately the responsibility of a smooth running production lies with you.

This might sound a little dramatic, but actually it's simply about assuming the role and making sure that prior to production you've considered all of the variables. Pre-production meetings help immensely in setting out your intentions and any concerns that might evolve in the shoot. Having an open dialogue with your client prior to production allows you to run a smooth shoot on the day.

Building good solid relations with your client, by working together in a consultative fashion, means that when things go wrong it doesn't become a huge deal. Just make sure you rectify the problem quickly and with the minimum of fuss. We are all human and things don't always go according to plan - people make mistakes - but when you have good relationships with clients these issues don't then become huge problems.

This approach will serve you well throughout each aspect of production. Everyone I have ever worked with understands that sometimes things go wrong, but it's how you handle these problems that separates you from your competition. If you charge premium prices, you need to offer a premium service.

A few years ago I was working with a coaching client (I don't take many people on like this these days, but I do occasionally if I think we're a good fit and they can afford my fees) and he wanted to learn more about filming with his DSLR gear and to up his skills one on one.

His ultimate plan was to learn from me and then go off and shoot his own corporate film for his business. We decided, however, after day one to turn the training session into the actual shoot for his corporate film. We shot it on his DSLR as he wanted to go through the workflow including recording the audio separately using dual audio (this was back in 2009). But when we came to edit, the audio plugin wouldn't sync the clips automatically. The result was a task that should have taken a few minutes, ended up taking three hours, while I manually synced the clips.

To the client, he'd lost three hours of editing time.

Obviously at the time I apologised for the delay, and said I would add on an extra half-day at my cost to make up for the three hour delay. I then followed up with email saying thank you for his time and that I apologise once again for the technical difficulties we had and that I'd add an additional half-day at my expense to grade the film and add some additional value to him in lieu of the situation.

He left very happy.

Running a successful business is about factoring in the downsides as much as the upsides. And when you factor in accountability, you will be adding maturity into your business.

Under Promise - Over Deliver

I mentioned earlier about the benefits of being a premium priced supplier which allows you to be focused on your client's needs without the distraction of multiple jobs happening simultaneously.

This enables me to be 100% reliable and never in a position where I'm letting them down. I've done some pretty big jobs in the last few years for Sony and they can be an extremely demanding client, however, this is only to be expected when they're investing in a premium service.

Whenever I'm creating a budget for a large corporate production, I always factor in allowances for unforeseen elements that could crop up throughout production; things can change and sometimes it's just not appropriate to re-quote because of this. The last thing you want to be doing is finding yourself in a position where you feel you've undercharged, especially when the client asks for additional support.

On the flipside, I tend to favour under promising and over delivering as a general approach in my corporate work.

Experience tells me that if I factor in all the resources required on any given project, and I think we can complete it in three days, based on the information I may have to hand, I'll likely tell the client to allow for *four days, in early discussions.* I find this approach helps to manage expectations well before shoot date. Then if we manage to do the shoot in three days, the client saves 25% and the perception is we've planned to be more efficient and were able to achieve more in less time.

Building in a contingency to each aspect of your production is a really good habit to get into, especially in the early stages of negotiation. It gives me a bit of headroom and puts me in a great position. When projects get under way things always grow - this is often known as *'scope creep'* I'll be talking more about 'scope creep' in the managing projects chapter. If you factored in a 25% headroom in your planning, you can then make the decision whether you need to re-quote or whether you can absorb the extra request without the perceived additional cost to the client. This can be great for relationship building and demonstrates that you are willing to be flexible, but in actual fact you've pre-empted the likelihood in advance and factored that into the original estimate. The result is, you look good to your client, but you don't lose out financially.

Focus on delivering value not on how much things cost.

Providing exceptional value to your clients is what you should be aiming for in your business. If you become a trusted partner and deliver exceptional value to your customers, the cost of your service becomes elastic. By that, I mean the client will be less focused on the *actual cost of doing business with you,* so long as you're delivering exceptional value.

As I progress my relations with my clients, I'm able to increase my prices based on the additional value I bring to a production. When you really love a service or product, you can get to a point where you want that service or product regardless of what it costs (remember my love for Macintosh products).

Apple computers are a perfect example of value against cost. I have been using Apple computers since 2004 and have many Macs and Apple products in both my business and personal life. I'm sure the Mac versus PC debate will not be unfamiliar to you. Fans of the PC will rightly claim that you can build a higher specified machine, with more functionality using PC components for much less money than the equivalent Mac. Yet I will not touch a PC so long as I live. Macs makes my life easier, which is why I spent $1000 on an iPhone when an equivalent Samsung would cost me less than half of that.

I was in New York in September 2014, on holiday with my wife, when the iPhone 6 was being released. I said to Sam how cool it would be if we could pick one up that weekend. The queues were four to five hours long for the main store on Broadway, so we decided in the end not to queue. In fact, a few days later, we passed another Apple store. The queues were still two hours long and I would have been willing to stand and wait had it not been for the fact that I couldn't buy an unlocked phone at that point. Interestingly, a few doors down the street there was a Samsung store that had a handful of people in it. They were offering free coffee, free pastries and soft drinks for kids. I decided to go and check it out. I honestly had an open mind about giving this phone a fair chance, because on spec, it's a very powerful mobile device. However, the second I picked it up and saw the interface, I put it right back down again. I realised that I am completely and utterly loyal to the iOS and the way the Apple interfaces make me feel.

So I'm willing to pay at least *twice the price* of competing brands for a device that doesn't necessarily have twice the functionality. But I still want it. I love Apple products, and they make my life easier.

This is an important lesson in value. I perceive Apple as making my life less stressful and more integrated. And the only thing that matters is my relationship with the brand and how it makes me feel. If you take the same concept and apply it to your relationships then you will provide a service that minimises stress, optimises your client's time when working on a filming projects, and they'll pay you more for the pleasure of it.

Focus your effort on becoming a trusted supplier to your clients; be that person they can rely on, who never lets them down.

Get yourself into that position and you can charge a premium rate for what you offer.

Clarify all discussions in writing

The media industry is renowned for verbal based agreements. When I was a freelance cameraman back in the early 2000s, I can't remember a situation where I actually signed a contract to take on work. Everything was done on phone and email.

My advice when running a production company, is to follow up any discussion on the phone *in writing*. Email is fine, just make sure you clarify any verbal discussions, summarising the points that were agreed and how you will be moving forward. If you're not already doing this, then start, because it helps avoid any confusion prior to the project taking place. It is particularly important when highlighting the parameters of a project and what is and is not included in your cost estimate.

The friendly nature of a consultative business works well for building relationships, but it's vitally important that you protect yourself where the primary purpose is to provide a service in return for payment. Every time I discuss a project with a client, many factors can be raised during the call so I always make handwritten notes throughout, then once we've finished I confirm everything in an email, summarising with bullet points anything that was agreed.

Taking this step to get the client to confirm or add points of their own, will be enough to help with any disputes in the future.

You're bound to experience a situation where the client has said one thing during a pre-production meeting, and then contradicts what they originally said when it comes to execution of that project. The best way to act in this situation is to politely suggest you refer back to the email where everything was written down.

This was a practice I adopted in the early days of tapeless workflows, when we'd always insist the production team email us the specifics of the frame rates and Codecs they wanted while on location. As soon as you have something in writing, you have something to refer back to when you get to post-production.

This method of logging phone calls and conversations has saved me and my reputation many times over. It's also just a good habit to get into; it avoids confusion and keeps clear communication between you and the client.

I can't emphasise enough how important this is; friendly relations can go sour very quickly if confusion about the outcome of a project is purely based on a conversation that wasn't logged (and clarified) by both parties.

Another thing that is very important to be clear about is the cost estimate process and exactly what is included in your quotation. This is especially important when it comes to post-production estimating. I will always estimate how many days I believe are required in post-production. Within that I will state the number of days of editing and also when I will need feedback and *consolidated notes* from the client. Notice I say *consolidated notes*, because often there can be more than one stakeholder involved in a project. You may be dealing with one or two people to begin with, but as soon as the film is taking shape, it's amazing how suddenly more and more people will have an opinion. It's very important you don't get sucked into multiple stakeholders sending you feedback for changes, which is why we specify *one set* of consolidated changes at a time. Normally on short corporate projects, I will factor in two rounds of changes within the cost estimate. I will also specify the timings that those feedback requests need to be submitted. The last thing you want as a production company is to be waiting for clients to come back to you.

I had a client project once where I was dealing with one key stakeholder, and once I had delivered the result of the film piece, he showed it to his partner. They were both very happy with the result. Until that point, the board had not been interested in the project. However upon seeing the film, suddenly there were six different people with an opinion and after two rounds of changes a further report was made asking for more. My response was simple: *"I'm very happy to make more changes, however, if you refer back to our original agreement you'll notice that the two rounds of changes and three days have already been used, and so there will be a further charge for each additional edit. This will be charged at £850 per day."* At which point the client referred back to the board and they decided the film was actually fine the way it was. However, if I had not put parameters in place and clearly stated what was included in the estimate, I could easily have been editing for days without additional payment from the client. If you allow this to happen, any profit margin you have factored in will be eroded very quickly. If there are additional changes you need to make it clear to the client that there will be additional charges.

So make sure you're clear with the client about what is and isn't included in your cost estimate. They will appreciate your honesty and hopefully no undue surprises will then occur.

Be Professional And Never Miss A Deadline

Being professional may sound obvious but it's worth emphasising. Those of us with an artistic temperament can find dealing with clients in corporate environments frustrating. It's usually the decision making stages of signing off on a project which can really slow it down.

You'll often find there can be great enthusiasm for a project in the initial stages, but if a key decision maker or stakeholder is on holiday or away from the business, things can grind to a halt. So I always try and set out a timeline *early on in the pre-production process,* and that includes deadlines so that you can progress the project.

Taking on the position as producer and overall project manager will allow you to maintain a production flow within your internal resources, but it also allows you to outline a timeline, with key milestones set out along the way.

It's a good working practice to set everything out in writing and map out the project to the client so that you both have a clear understanding of what will happen and when. *That way you can bring the project in on time and within budget.* The last thing you want is any delays from a client, especially if it involves a delay in getting paid. It's also important to have things documented to avoid confusion and maintain a good professional relationship throughout production.

Chapter 9
HOW TO SELL

Have Confidence In Your Offer

Selling is a subject that can really freak out filmmakers and creatives. I'm not really sure why, because selling is an art form and it can be very creative. However, there are certain aspects to selling that must be applied in order for it to become less daunting.

First of all, you have to have *confidence* in what you're offering. You cannot go out and sell a service you're not capable of delivering. Nor should you sell a premium service at a premium rate if you can't deliver it. You don't expect the same level of service in economy as those travelling in first class.

Having confidence in your offer equates to you having given consideration to every aspect of the service you intend to provide. Once this has been clarified and you've handled your pre-client meetings properly, you will have all the information that you need to best match the clients' needs.

Andrew's story

I was on a coaching call a few days ago with Andrew, a filmmaker from Aberdeen. We were discussing an opportunity he had, and he wanted to know if there would be any value in him taking it up.

Here's the scenario; there was to be a large martial arts exhibition in Glasgow. Andrew was thinking of going along to see if he could drum up any business as he is moving into producing videos for martial arts businesses and schools. My advice was to offer some free 'on the day' short promo videos for the event exhibitors. He was apprehensive, but after some encouragement, he felt he had nothing to lose.

He did, and what happened next was nothing short of brilliant...

He not only made short videos, but he took photos of their booths which he uploaded there and then, the exhibitors were blown away. They got video and stills the same day. And in return, Andrew asked to be considered if they ever needed any video shooting.

But it didn't stop there. A well-known martial arts expert was speaking at the event and Andrew offered to shoot his talk. After filming the speech he offered to upload 15 minutes of this talk for free, and if he wanted the rest, he would have to commit to using his company for their next corporate film.

He agreed.

Andrew estimates that the minimum return on that one day would exceed £10,000 worth of new business. And since that event he has been approached by more companies who were exhibiting.

During our initial coaching call, Andrew had expressed concern at 'putting himself out there', and he is not alone in that feeling because if you are stepping outside of your comfort zone you are going to come up against resistance from your subconscious.

Selling can be uncomfortable if you are not used to it and unsure of how to proceed, but like anything in life, if you want to achieve extraordinary success, sometimes you have to step out of your comfort zone.

The difference in confidence in Andrew's voice from one coaching call to the next was incredible. He simply applied what I taught him, took a deep breath, and then stepped into an arena where he had nothing to lose, and did incredibly well.

I've only spoken to Andrew twice on coaching calls, but I can tell that he has the necessary tenacity and belief in his own products to succeed, and he will build a thriving video business.

What was especially interesting was that a stills photographer approached him at the trade show and said, *"What are you doing uploading images to the web from the show? You are stealing our business."*

However, I would argue that the marketplace is open to anyone who is prepared to do what's required to win the business. I'm certain that photographer had the means to upload images from his digital camera to the web in exactly same way Andrew did, but most likely he couldn't be bothered (or hadn't thought of the idea). I'm proud to say Andrew won hands down and you could too if you are prepared to do it.

Another really important aspect to having confidence in your offer is being prepared to walk away. Now this may not be something you feel very comfortable with when starting out, but if you are more established then you have to know what your *'walk away'* point is. (Remember, the person willing to walk away is the person with all the power.)

Always keep in mind that you're running a business to make a profit and it makes no sense whatsoever to do a job when someone is trying to hack you down on price. If you remember, I spoke earlier about the importance of how you discount based on adding value, not money off. There are always clients who are willing to pay you what you're worth, but equally there are clients who are not. My advice is; *build your business towards attracting more of the clients who play by your rules and sack the ones who don't.*

When you reach a point in your business where you are willing to walk away from work, you gain incredible power on many levels. Not only does it help you to relax and avoid getting into business deals with people who don't respect you, but it will give you an air of confidence that will unsettle a client who thinks they can get work on the cheap. On numerous occasions I have said to a client, *"if you cannot afford this that's okay"*, because I know I'm not the cheapest supplier and nor do I want to be.

Letting potential clients know that you are willing to walk away is known as 'takeaway selling'. By demonstrating that you can be very discerning with which offers you accept puts you in a very powerful position and it gives you the freedom to work with clients who do value your service.

Remember; your business, *your rules.*

People Buy From People

The single most important part of selling is understanding you're selling to a person, and people *buy from people.* I've spoken a lot about the importance of relationships, and this is especially important at the point of sale. I've already talked about the importance of becoming a consultative friend who makes life easy for your clients. When it comes to making the sale, it's important that you've established this relationship and reiterated how much value you are going to bring to the project. More importantly, how much hassle you are going to remove from the project and how much easier your client's life will be, when working with you.

So when you are discussing a project with the client, or indeed the estimate of costs, remind them of this aspect. In most cases, clients just need to be educated so they can understand the daily cost attached to using that service.

For example, we offer an archiving service that goes beyond the footage living on a hard drive. Hard drives are not guaranteed, and we have invested in an archiving system that uses LTO tape. Now beyond the cost of this (which is approximately $30 per tape), we have invested an infrastructure that safeguards the clients assets. So when it comes to explaining that we've invested in excess of $5000 in that area of our business, the client understands why we charge $100 for archiving services. It's a simple cost versus benefit equation and when we explain to the client that we are the experts in managing this kind of data, which in turn takes the risk of losing data out of *their hands,* they are much more likely to accept the charges.

As a side note, this method of storing clients' work means you can guarantee its safety, but if the client wants to re-version the footage, then you are more likely to get the work. At the very least, you can charge them a 'withdraw fee' when they request their footage from the library.

Clients that you get to know very well will hopefully, over time, become strong business friendships. I recall working with one particular marketing manager who became a good friend. It got to the point where when he required a video he would get on the phone and say, *"Hey Den, I need a video shooting; it needs to be three minutes and cover X,Y and Z. I've got £15,000 allocated, if you think that's enough cool, if not let me know and I can see if I can find some more money".* And because of our relationship, the trust associated, and level of understanding between us, it usually became a win-win for us both. This level of trust in a relationship has gone a long way in both personal and business friendships. I'm not interested in quick wins at the expense of longevity. Taking the time to build relations and develop mature business associations is very worthwhile for the long-term success of my business.

The media industry especially has a large community aspect running throughout it. Having worked in the broadcast TV industry for some years, I'm continually surprised how many people I know - who started off as runners and production coordinators - are now directors, producers, production managers and even TV execs. The same is true in the corporate world; I've worked with junior account execs at agencies who are now in more senior positions. In fact, someone I used to work with 10 years ago is now in a very senior position in the marketing and advertising department of major petroleum company. Now, I'm not really interested in that kind of work at the moment, but if that was a direction I wanted to take my business in, I know I could get a meeting and I'm confident we would more than likely get a chance to pitch for some significant budget projects.

So, remember, people buy from people and if you build strong relationships from the very get go, you never know where you might come across that person again, and in what position they could be in to help you in your journey.

Listen, listen, listen

Fact! The more you listen and the more you understand the deep root of the pain a client suffers, the more money you will make.

You have to ask lots of questions to really understand the clients problem, or what it is they want to achieve.

Remember the story I told you about the company which sold theft protection, and originally wanted a CSI style production? Well, it wasn't until I really listened to their issue that we came up with something a lot more beneficial to them, and I urge you to do the same for your clients.

Building a solid relationship can turn into profit; the more you keep in touch, and the more you listen, the more you can pick up about their budget plans for the next year and what other projects may be on the horizon. If you are routinely in contact with that person and you take a genuine interest in their plans, it's more likely you will be on their radar.

From experience, clients don't always know what they want, plus they often change their minds. Fully understanding the client's goals and their own internal challenges can arm you with valuable information to help pitch a fully encompassing solution that will take all of their clients pain away.

Only when you've gathered all of the information can you then go away and put together a comprehensive proposal based on listening to the client and asking all of the right questions.

When to present the price

It's very important to know exactly when the right moment is to present your cost estimate.

Never give a price before you have all the facts, regardless of how much the client pushes you.

I hear many horror stories where a client phones up, asks for the price and is given one there and then. You can't price a project without having all the facts. You need to have a solid understanding of what will be involved before you start talking about money.

The three key areas of estimating a job

Generally speaking, when I present a budget to a client, I send a covering letter that outlines what has been discussed, the scope of the project and the details of the key objectives that the client laid out.

I then break the estimate down into three key areas: **Pre-production, Production** and **Post-production**, with separate itemised costings for each segment of the estimate.

In my experience, once you present an estimate of costs, it's very rare for that figure to be increased. So the reason you want to present your price as late as possible, is that once you announce that figure, it can only ever go down. You have to be certain that you've factored in *all the likely costs* for your production and allowed for aspects that may creep out of your control. It's also very important at the estimate stage, that you clarify what is and is not included, especially when it comes to post-production days and revisions. Each job will be different and to some degree some elements may be difficult to schedule until you know what's been shot. You must factor in some contingency into your estimate so you don't end up doing more work than you're actually being paid to do.

It is also worth documenting that the estimate is just that; an estimate, and that final billing may be higher due to unforeseen costs. Although in practice, like I mentioned previously, the likelihood of getting more money from a client is extremely rare so make sure you factor in enough contingency. I do a great deal of work overseas and clients are often asking for estimates of costs in advance of travel and accommodation being booked. So what I tend to do is get an approximation of what those travel costs may be and I factor in a 10 or 15% increase, so that I'm not ending up out of pocket.

Additionally, if I book travel in advance and I don't get paid for 60 days, then I'm going to be incurring interest charges on my credit card, which can run into hundreds of pounds. So it's smart to factor that into your cost estimate, so that it doesn't end up coming off your bottom line, which eats into your profit and your morale.

It's not that I believe in withholding the price per se, it's more about controlling when I give that information over to the client. I don't want to have a client make preconceived decisions on price without fully understanding the true value of what it is they are getting in return for their investment. It's just human nature to want to know how much something is going to cost and actually it's far easier to make a balanced decision on the true worth of investment once you have a clear outline of everything that is involved.

I am no psychologist but I know enough about dealing with people in a sales situation that if they feel that your offer provides great value (even if it seems expensive compared to what they might normally spend) then they will find a way to meet the estimate.

Offering incentives when delivering an estimate

I generally don't like offering discounts; instead I prefer to offer incentives to clients as a way of leveraging cash flow. For example, some clients might react to an estimate with, *"it's a bit more than I wanted to spend,"* to which my first response is, *"okay, what is the figure you are trying to reach?"* If it's within three to five % of the overall budget, I may offer them a chance to use early payments as a leveraging tool.

Let's say a corporate client normally pays between 60 to 90 days then I may offer a three to five % reduction of the cost if they make a payment within 30 days. In most cases the clients don't have much control over the accounting procedures - particularly in larger corporations - but I have used this to effect on smaller jobs where I prefer to have the cash paid quicker and reduce the overall budget.

A clever way to deliver cost savings to a client is to bundle your services and offer an overall price for multiple services. Below is an example.

A client calls you to discuss filming a project. When you ask about how this will be edited, they tell you they will probably use their usual editor but they have not yet confirmed if they are available, and so invite you to quote, asking for a separate quote for shooting and editing.

Here's how I would present this to a client;

Option a) you deliver a quote for shooting only, at a cost of £2000.

Option b) you deliver a quote for editing:

    3 days of offline editing at £850 per day =£2250

    5 hrs online editing at £200 per hour £1000

    5 hrs grading at £200 per hour £1000

    Sub Total Post = £4550

If they use two suppliers independently, it will cost a total of £6550 for the shoot and edit.

But (and here is where you can leverage your services, while making the client feel good about the deal) you say, *"If you do post-production with us, in addition to the shooting, we'll discount the online editing and grading by 50%"* and then you offer those 'value added services' at the discounted rate of £100 per hour.

The client saves £1000 overall by bundling the shooting and post-production with you.

Total cost to them is £5550, if they use a single supplier.

The best part is you're not really losing any money because online editing and grading is a finishing process that only happens if you win the edit.

So it's like an upsell.

Some clients like to have an option a, b, and c. It's a bit like when you're flying on a plane; economy, business or first-class. Different people respond to different price points and there is no reason why you can't offer different levels of service, especially to a new client where you're gauging the level of likely spend.

Remember, if you're looking to offer a full service, then it's your job to explain to the client that you're offering a high value service. Don't undersell yourself just to try and win the work. Be very careful about applying your own perceptions of money and wealth onto your cost estimates. Never EVER base your pricing on what you think is *'fair'* or *'reasonable'*, or worse still, keeping in line with *'industry standard'*.

The pitfalls of industry standard pricing

The term *'industry standard'* is the very worst statement you can ever make to yourself and your business. Industry standard simply means the MINIMUM standard at which most businesses operate in a particular niche. Notice the emphasis on *minimum*. You don't want to be *'minimum'* on any level, and particularly not when it comes to your business.

> *If you don't feel a little uncomfortable when you present your estimate or price for your service, then you're not charging enough.*

Why on earth you would want to be working at the minimal level with the rest of the bottom feeders? My approach to business is all about *'premier positioning'*, *'premium services'* and *'premium pricing'* to match. I don't care what other people are charging. If you believe you are competing with another business on price, then you need to look closely at how you're running your business and work on repositioning it.

This is one of the most uncomfortable topics for many creatives and filmmakers to get their head around, because most filmmakers want to be liked and don't want to stand out from the crowd.

If you want to grow your business and make money, you need to think differently and you need to start by getting comfortable with feeling uncomfortable about your pricing and how much money you are going to charge a client for your exceptional service.

Like I say, never ever base your pricing on what you think is reasonable. You can never predict how much budget a client really has to make a video. So it's far better to pitch your pricing at the higher end of where you think it needs to be - allowing some flexibility. You can always adjust the price down, but you can never start low and go up.

Sell The Avoidance Of Pain

We are far more motivated away from pain than we are in the gaining of pleasure. Your clients want to have an easy life, whilst getting a great product that serves the purposes outlined in your initial meetings. When you know what pain your clients are suffering (from a film production point of view) it's then just a simple exercise to explain how you can alleviate it.

I can explain this using the analogy of the discomfort I experience with my arthritic ankle. Occasionally I have to apply pain relief with either cream or tablets. When the pain is really severe simple aspirin or paracetamol have little effect, so I then look for tablets specifically targeting arthritis pain. The cost is irrelevant. I literally don't care if those products are five times the cost of standard paracetamol, I just want the pain to go away quickly. It becomes an emotional decision to remove the pain as quickly as possible and therefore I'm willing to pay five times more.

If you apply this same principle, you can then be the 100% pain relief solution to your clients' pain.

If you start to look at client projects and identify the weakness or the vulnerabilities the client is facing, you can help to make them stronger. This is not about exploiting pain but solving problems and supporting your clients so they become better with you as a result.

The reason for emphasising the solving of pain is because most filmmakers worry too much about what other filmmakers will think, and spend too much time trying to be nice in the hope that the client will use them. It might take you a while to get your head around this notion of relieving pain, but take my word for it, accept it and think about how you can use it going forwards.

Remember the story I told you back on page 92? If you can't, then I suggest you go back and re-read. It's a valuable lesson in taking away a client's pain, and offering a service that will benefit the them.

Chapter 10
MANAGING YOUR JOBS EFFECTIVELY

Pre-production Is Where You Make A Film

Pre-production is where many filmmakers fail to charge enough or they don't build in adequate allowance into their cost estimates. The pre-production stage - if done comprehensively - can be labour intensive and time consuming.

Pre-production can include:

- Identifying and booking crew
- Equipment requirements
- Logistics and access
- Location recce
- Scripting and shot lists
- Production run down and call sheets
- Developing the creative brief
- General client admin

This list may not seem extensive but you can see how many hours (if not days) this part of production could consume. And whether or not you have someone employed full-time, or you do this yourself, the client needs to understand what these tasks are and that they need to be actioned prior to production taking place.

Let's look at each of these key topics in detail

1) Identifying and booking crew

You will no doubt have people you like to work with. Perhaps they have a great attitude or they are really good at what they do, but this creates a problem; they are generally in demand, so it's likely that your 'go to crew' may not always be available and you may have to use your B team. This process alone can take a couple of days, especially if they are on location working on other productions. The very nature of a freelance market is that your team are likely to be busy doing other things. (Don't forget once you've booked a crew you need to inform them of the production dates and locations. Then once the job is complete, manage receipt of their invoices and process payment along with the associated accounting tasks.)

2) Equipment requirements

Understanding what you'll need for the specific production - including any additional lighting grip or sound equipment - will take some planning. It may be that you are keen to try and utilise your own resources, which is a time saver, however you may need to employ the services of a kit hire company or cross hire equipment from your crew. Either way, this process takes time. You have to plan what you need, then you have to make a reservation with a kit hire company.

If you don't already have a relationship with an equipment hire company, then you will have to set up an account, which takes time and requires trade references. More importantly, you can't hire gear without insurance.

You also have to bear in mind that if you rent equipment, the chances are the terms and conditions of that company will mean that you have to pay your invoice within 30 days, and if the client isn't paying you for 60 or 90 days, then you need to make sure you have cash flow for any third party rentals. If you know the client is not going to pay you for 60 or 90 days and you are liable for any equipment hire, then essentially you're bankrolling the client's production. Therefore, it is very important that you negotiate good rates with your rental company and charge an additional percentage to your client for financing the equipment.

On larger jobs, I always insist on a 50% upfront payment to limit my liability. If you can cash flow it, then it's an opportunity to make an additional margin on equipment hire. For instance, most rental companies will give you a reasonable discount off their list price so if the client starts asking what this cost is, refer them to the 'rack rates' (what the supplier lists their prices as) of the rental company (which are the prices you're charging), while getting the kit for 20 to 30% less, thus making you a 20 to 30% margin on the equipment hire.

Just remember, as the project evolves, the requirements for equipment often change which means you have to follow up and modify the kit list. This all takes time and needs to be charged for within your cost estimate. I normally absorb this into the 20 to 30% margin I make on kit hire.

3) Logistics and access

Wherever you plan to film, there will be some form of permit or permission requirement. Even if the location does not charge a fee, it is likely they will want to see evidence of public liability insurance, which usually needs to be between two and five million pounds. You then have to consider the logistics of a given location: can you get easy access? If equipment needs to be carried, can be done safely and in a way that minimises heavy lifting for the crew?

As a producer you need to ensure that you make the practical aspects of getting to location safe for all people involved. Health and safety is a legal responsibility of the producer and part of that process is careful assessment of the location.

4) Location recce

In some cases, you may need to go to a location to assess

practicalities (mentioned on the previous page) but also to consider things like available light, power and physical space. Some clients are reluctant to pay for location scouting and recce days but it's worth explaining to them that the value in factoring in a recce day means your DP (if available) can assess how much lighting is required, how accessible power and other amenities are and therefore have a much more informed view of what will be needed. The alternative is to order more lighting, grip and equipment because without seeing the location, you just can't be certain what you'll need. When I explain this to clients they generally understand that a specific recce can save them money in the long run.

5) Scripting and shot lists

Breaking down the shoot day into a script and or shot lists is another important part of pre-production planning. Executing a well organinsed pre-production plan will speed things up on the shoot day. Again, depending on the size of production, this process can take a few hours or several days. But as it's a real benefit to the client, then you need to factor in the time spent doing this. Scripting will also involve sending drafts to the client for approval, and this can also take time. Just be aware, as more people become involved in the process on the client side, things can change multiple times and you need to factor this into your costs.

6) Production run down and call sheets

Once everything has been set up and a plan has been agreed, you then need to create a production run down which clearly maps out what will be done and when. If you don't carefully plan your time on shoot day, you could end up running over. If your crew are on a fixed 10 or 12 hour day and you do this, then you could be liable for overtime and the chances are the client will not be footing the bill. To avoid overages like this, careful planning in pre-production will minimise any risk. Your crew will happily help you out on the odd occasion, but do it too many times and they'll soon start refusing to work with you unless they're getting paid additional amounts for longer days.

The call sheet is a *vital document* that explains to everyone involved in the production what's happening on the day, what time people are expected on location, any details on parking, transportation, safety, and arrangements for subsistence. The call sheet also details start and end times for the shoot day and often a brief outline of what will be filmed and who is required.

Call sheets take a lot longer to prepare than you think and you might find producing one which involves five to 10 people will take you two to three hours. Then you have to make sure everyone receives the call sheet in advance of production.

If you would like to see an example of what the call sheet looks like then simply head over to www.businessforfilmmakers.com/callsheet

7) Developing the creative brief

The creativity aspect and concepts you bring to the brief have value but they are often difficult for clients to comprehend because they are intangible. In order to come up with a creative concept you need to spend time drawing on your own knowledge, creativity and experience. You will spend time thinking and researching and likely work on different versions of a brief. You can charge for this in two ways. You can either put a line item in for creative development or factor in a margin across other aspects of your production. I have used both methods and I tend to decide which one is most appropriate depending on the level of understanding the client has on the creative process.

8) General client admin

Finally, don't underestimate how much time you will spend in pre-planning meetings with the client, be it in person, on the phone, or over email. As an experiment, I noted down every time I was in communication with the client throughout a production and it's frightening how much time can be sucked out of you during a project. This is another reason why I favour the premium pricing mode which allows me to only work with one client at a time. That way I can dedicate all my time and focus on *that* project. This can become a very stressful part of a project especially if you're waiting on people to get back to you and a client is being indecisive about what they actually want.

I hope the eight key sections here have illustrated how much work is involved in this first stage of production. What is alarming is how few filmmakers charge appropriately for this aspect of production.

You're doing the work, therefore you should be charging for it.

Have 2 Budgets

This is a very important aspect of running a production, and one you have to keep a close eye on. It's very simple; you have your actual **hard costs in one budget** and you have what you're **charging the client in another**. Let's say you charge the client £450 per day for the camera package, but the rental house is only charging you £350. Having those figures in separate budgets allows you to calculate your overall gross margin for the project.

If you want to make a good profit in production, you have to be firm in making a margin on *every aspect of the production* you can. Remember, there is nothing wrong with being friendly to your clients, but you are delivering them a service and you should be making a profit for that. Continually referring to your 'working budget' will keep you in a safe position for maintaining your margin. If you don't keep an eye on this, costs can quickly spiral out of control.

Also, certain aspects of production can come in under or over what was budgeted for, and so having an overall tally on a spreadsheet will often mean that if you go over in some segments and under in another, you'll maintain a positive position overall.

I recall one project, where I had estimated the cost for a location fixer at £350 per day, but when we got the invoice it was somewhat higher at nearly £500, purely down to unforeseen costs on location. I had budgeted £400 per day for the client budget, thinking it was costing me £350, but in actual fact I was a £100 out of pocket per day on that line item. However, I'd made some economies on other aspects of the production, plus the hotels had not come in quite as expensive as I'd estimated, so I was able to offset the loss against these, which balanced my production budget.

Parking and incidentals are other sneaky expenses that can really mount up, so make sure you factor in a generous amounts to cover them. Clients will understand if you explain this to them. In some parts of London, parking can be as much as £20 per hour, that can be *£160 per day* for an eight hour shooting day. Be careful not to get caught out.

So, have two budgets. Just make sure the client doesn't see the hard cost budget – not that it's any of their business - but you don't want them seeing where you're making your profit margins!

Write everything down

To manage production effectively, it's important that you *document everything*. I use a variety of tools to do this. I use **Google Drive** and do my budgeting using the spreadsheet function, and it stores everything on the cloud. I also like the fact that I can share documents with other members of the production team and we can work on them simultaneously. This is particularly useful at the planning stage.

I often work with James Tonkin from Hangman Studios in London and we both have very busy schedules. Add to the fact that we live 80 miles apart, so meeting face to face is virtually impossible. So when we are planning productions together, we jump on **Skype** and simultaneously work on a document on Google Drive. (If you're not familiar with Google Drive, multiple stakeholders can simultaneously work in one document and it updates live, as opposed to having multiple versions of a hardcopy document that gets sent around and can get very confusing.) Google Drive also has a number of other very useful features including **Google Calendar** which can be set up as a production-based calendar where you can invite key stakeholders in, and they can update and manage that calendar as well. For me, the shared workspace that Google Drive offers is absolutely fantastic. You can even use Google hangouts to hold production meetings.

Another tool I use religiously is **Evernote** (evernote.com). I manage all of my productions and details within Evernote. In fact, I manage most of my life in Evernote. Evernote is like a virtual filing cabinet where I have a notebook for each client job, and I store all of the information for that project within it. This is particularly useful in pre-production where sometimes projects can take a while to materialise, and rather than relying on searching for email trails, I simply cut and paste conversations and developments into notebooks in Evernote.

The final key resource that I use is **Dropbox** (dropbox.com). Dropbox is simply cloud-based file storage where I can share project assets with clients and stakeholders alike.

I use these three cloud-based services predominantly to run most of my productions. Google Drive is free with a Gmail account, Dropbox and Evernote are a subscription-based service and are very affordable.

Managing cash during production

I mentioned earlier that you should have two budgets, a client budget and a working budget, but I also advise having a *cash flow management spreadsheet* for every production. Now on smaller productions you may not feel this is necessary.

We made a film a couple of years ago for Sony and we had a cast and crew of 12, with five vehicles and 12 people to feed for three days. This also included various people during pre-production, production and post, and petty cash was being spent on parking, fuel, travel, subsistence and other incidentals which soon added up. I actually created a daily cash spend spreadsheet on that production and kept a close eye on all the petty cash that was being spent. You would be surprised how quickly it all mounts up: parking, transportation and feeding people. You just need to be keeping an accurate track of where money is being spent, otherwise it can be eating into your own margin.

One thing I am very clear about in my productions is that we provide accurate *parking instructions* on the call sheet (which we identify on the recce) and we make clear that individuals are responsible for their *own parking*, but will be reimbursed by production on presentation of a receipt. **Under no circumstances** will we accept liability for parking fines. You need to make your crew responsible for the safe and secure parking of their vehicles. The last thing you need or want is to be facing parking fines that could easily have been avoided. Clear instruction on the call sheet eliminates this problem.

It's very easy for costs to run away from you when you're busy on production, but if you allow this to happen then you're only eating into your own profit margin, so make this an important priority in your day when on location.

Mark up everything

If you are taking on the production role as a producer of content and effectively acting as an agency for a client, then you need to make sure that you are charging a percentage on top of every service you subcontract.

Every crew member should have a minimum of 10 to 20% added to the cost that they invoice you for. If you hire someone for £250 per day, then you want to be charging between £275 and £300 per day to the client.

We've already spoken about renting equipment, and you want to be negotiating a 20 to 30% discount off rack rate from the supplier but charging full rate to the client, thus factoring in a 20 to 30% profit margin for you. If you book any form of travel on behalf of the client, either getting crew to location or paying for accommodation, then factor in 10% or 20% on top as an admin charge. If you source music for the client then make sure you add a margin on top of that as well.

Remember, you're providing a service which involves you sourcing on behalf of your client, so it's perfectly acceptable to add a margin on top.

Naturally, when you provide any service, factoring in a margin is what makes you profit. Having a great relationship with your suppliers can help you negotiate discounts, especially if you bring a certain volume of work to that supplier.

If you own your own equipment which you use on the shoot, then don't *'throw the gear in for free'* but charge a figure for your equipment in line with the cost if you would have to go and rent it.

If you are currently running a production company then go and have a look at your last few estimates. If you're bringing in suppliers and charging them out at cost, add a 10% or 20% margin on top. *This will instantly increase your profit margin by that amount in the next 12 months.*

Insurance, Liability And Legal Costs

Do not ignore this. If you are facilitating production you have a legal responsibility to keep everyone involved (including the general public) safe. As the producer you are *completely responsible for the health and safety aspect of both your crew and the public.*

I will not entertain a production without taking out comprehensive production insurance and public and employers' liability. Production insurance covers: production, the media assets, and if anything goes wrong production insurance generally covers the cost of an entire reshoot.

Legal Disclaimer: I am not an insurance professional and you should take proper insurance advice from a certified insurance broker specialising in the media industry. (You can get some recommendations over on www.businessforfilmmakers.com/ resources.)

You also *must have public liability in place.* This insurance doesn't cost as much as you might think, but don't forget you're passing this cost to the client anyway, so don't scrimp on this aspect.

If a member of the public trips over an item of your equipment, *they could sue.* And in this instance, the client will not want to get involved. This is your responsibility. Solid health and safety assessment backed up with professional crew, and a reputable public liability insurance policy, will minimise your liability. If someone gets injured, or worse killed, a court is going to want to know if adequate procedures were put in place and as the producer you are liable. This is actually true of any film production, no matter if it's professional or a bunch of students making a project.

Keeping your cast and crew safe at all times is your duty and legal responsibility. If you get this wrong you can end up in jail. The first A.D and producers who were on the shoot when Sarah Jones (Midnight Rider) was killed, are all facing corporate manslaughter charges. Granted that is an extreme case, but you must maintain a safe working environment *at all times* during shooting.

Take adequate legal advice when employing people, setting out contracts of employment and any other aspect of production that you think may require some legal counsel. I am a member of the FSB (Federation of Small Businesses) in the UK, and as part of my annual membership I have access to a free legal helpline. They have assisted me in the past with contracts for employment and other legal enquiries. Depending on where you live there may be an organisation that will help you in a similar way.

No client is ever going to take the risk of saying *"take the line-item of insurance off the estimate"*. Naturally, whatever this costs you, make sure you add your margin on top.

Maintain good clear and concise communication

I've never yet been on a production where things haven't changed as the shooting days progress. Things always go wrong, the weather can play its part and shoots almost always take longer than expected. Maintaining clear and concise communication with your client is a very wise strategy. Having a client on location with you, who is the decision maker, can be a very valuable asset when you hit a crossroads during a production day. Having someone with the decision making authority who can assess a problem with you and make a decision there and then about which best route to take, can save you an awful lot of aggravation.

There are only so many things you can prepare for, and explaining this to a client in advance of a production day is good practice. It always comes down to how well you're prepared and how well you develop your relationship with the client.

Adequate pre-production will mean that you will have given some thought to all the things that could possibly go wrong, and it's very prudent to have a plan B up your sleeve.

Comprehensive planning will always minimise the impact on a shoot if things don't quite go according to plan. This is true of most aspects of your business.

Prepare for the worst-case scenario and you'll always be pleasantly surprised.

Chapter 11
FINANCES, CASH FLOW & GETTING PAID

Setting Out Your Terms Of Business

It's one thing to win a client and work, but it can be a whole different thing getting paid. Setting out a simple one-page 'terms of agreement' can protect you. I'm not qualified to give legal advice so I encourage you to seek professional advice when setting up your own terms of business.

In simple terms, you just need to write down clearly and concisely what you will and won't be responsible for when you're engaged with the client project.

This can be very useful for clarifying terms and conditions, particularly around edits and revisions.

I recall speaking with a filmmaker recently who took our 'How to Shoot Sequences' program and he found himself in a situation where the client kept wanting more and more changes. Because they hadn't been clear from the outset, the client rightly assumed that unlimited changes were included in the price. If you do not specify exactly what is and is not included in your cost estimate, then you can't blame the client when they want repeat changes.

The net result for this filmmaker was that he was now making additional changes that had not been budgeted for, which was costing him money.

The best and clearest way to avoid any confusion is to specify any terms of business that you normally include, as well as two rounds of changes per offline edit, with specifics detailed on the cost estimate.

There is no reason why you can't modify your terms of business based on the specific client project, but it probably makes more sense to have standard business terms and any amendments or specific details highlighted in an attachment to the quote.

In addition to detailing any specific project and production parameters, e.g. who is supplying the location, who is providing music, and who is providing graphics, etc., the terms of business should clearly state the payment terms. On larger projects, I always insist on a 50% upfront payment if there are significant production costs to be borne by us. As I've already discussed, some clients will pay on 60 or 90 days, and you have to pay your crew on 30. You may also have to pay for other *'out of pocket'* production costs upfront.

On some projects, there may be split payments that go beyond simply 50% upfront. Every project is different but it is important that you have your payment terms laid out in detail in advance of the project commencing.

It's also important to note that the cost estimate is simply that, a cost 'estimate', and that you should have a clause that clearly states actual expenses may be higher, but will be discussed with the client during production for approval.

I use this exact phrase on my cost estimates:

"Estimate is valid for seven days from the date of issue. Fees and expenses quoted are for the original job description and layouts only, and for the usage specified. Final billing will reflect actual expenses. A purchase order or signed estimate and 50% of the estimate total is due upon booking. All rights not specifically granted in writing, including copyright, remain the exclusive property of Den Lennie."

By getting a client to sign the document, you have something that you can later rely on should there be any dispute.

I'm happy to report that in all my years of working in this industry, I've never had cause to dispute an invoice with a client. I put that down to clear and concise communication at all times, as well as having built a great relationship with them.

Any dispute that arises will largely be down to a lack of clear and concise communication.

I have used a couple of different legal contract services which are detailed at www.businessforfilmmakers.com/contracts and these have been particularly useful because you can simply buy an off-the-shelf contract and then pay an additional fee to have it double checked by one of the legal team in that company. I also mentioned earlier the FSB, which has a legal helpline should you need further support.

Finally, running your business as a sole trader is okay if you want to remain in the lower earning bracket of what is possible, but if you want to be taken seriously, you really need to set up a limited company and apply for a VAT registration number in the UK and Europe, or the GST in other parts of the world.

Running a limited company has several benefits, not least your liability is limited in the event of a financial claim on your company. If the company is limited, you are not personally liable for any debt and so your house and personal assets will always be protected.

The second huge benefit of being a limited company with VAT or GST registration is that you look like a bigger organisation. Nothing says one-man-band working in a bedroom than sole trader status.

If you're worried that accountant costs are going to get higher by changing your sole trader status, then you should be charging more money for your services. Plus your accountant – if they are doing their job properly – should be saving you on tax, at least to the equivalent of their costs, so their fees will be absorbed.

Setting Up Trade And Supplier Accounts

Once you win a contract, the decision maker may not have any direct influence in the accounting procedure of that business and these can be very particular and take time to set up.

Different companies and organisations have different requirements when setting up a supplier account. Some larger organisations insist on a signed document being sent in the post. For example, when I work with companies in Asia, they always require a signed hard copy invoice. And when I set up my supplier account with Sony in Japan, they required a signature mailed to them with the account application form. Setting up accounts can take months in some cases, and every company has a different procedure.

Larger organisations will only accept an invoice once an appropriate purchase order has been submitted.

Some clients insist on a quote being submitted first, then they will issue a purchase order and then when you raise your invoice the purchase order details must be correctly formatted on the invoice, otherwise it will be rejected. Always read the small print and comply with each different accounts procedure. People who work in accounts rarely know what service you have supplied, they just meticulously check the details and they will delay payment if procedures have not been followed.

While working with larger organisations can often mean larger production budgets and resulting sums of money being involved, the caveat is that you will probably have to jump through more hoops and red tape to actually get paid.

Make sure you factor in the time to get set up correctly on a payment system with a new client. You have to get to grips with how the client's payment system works.

Many larger companies are now outsourcing the financing and payments to centralised businesses, which are external to the organisation hiring you, so you have to be very careful to follow the instructions on the purchase order, to ensure there is no delay in receiving payment.

Ultimately you need to make it easy for your clients to pay you. For instance, if you work with foreign companies, you should have multiple currency bank accounts, and make sure all of the banking details are clearly identified on your invoices.

Nothing frustrates me more - when I'm paying a supplier – than an invoice which doesn't clearly show all the relevant banking information (including the IBAN number and Swift code). Make sure you have all your banking details clearly visible on your payment invoice along with your business registration number and your VAT or GST tax number.

If you are a non-US business supplying US businesses you will likely need to fill out a W-8 Ben form or W-9 form (both are taxation declaration forms) and these must be submitted prior to any invoice being paid. All of this takes time to set up.

When I did a job recently for Ralph Lauren in the US, their standard policy meant that from the point of initial discussion to payment took over 72 days.

If you need to rent equipment then you'll more than likely need to set up a trade account. This will take some time, as they will require a copy of your insurance that specifies the coverage of rented equipment as well as two trade references. If you are new to that company, they will likely require full payment in advance until you build up a good credit rating. Also, your insurance needs to cover loss of hire should you break or lose anything.

This is yet another reason why incorporating a limited liability company is so vital.

Hire a bookkeeper

When you run a limited company you have a legal responsibility as a director to maintain good accounting records. One of the first employees I hired in my business was a bookkeeper. I say employee but in actual fact she is a freelance bookkeeper who we have on a part-time basis. Every receipt and invoice that comes in and out of the business passes through her hands and she keeps a very accurate record of all movements of finances.

When we first became an incorporated company we were not VAT registered, but we very quickly hit the threshold and therefore became VAT registered (value added tax is like GST or sales tax and currently stands at £81,000 turnover per annum in the UK). One of the benefits of being VAT registered is that you can reclaim VAT on items you have purchased up to four years prior to registration on goods, and six months for services (as of Oct 2014). We had bought a large amount of computer and filmmaking equipment and so our first return showed the VAT office owing *us money*. You can elect to be VAT registered even if you don't hit the threshold. Don't be intimidated by charging VAT, especially if you make films for corporate and industrial applications.

However, if you shoot weddings, then adding 20% tax to every estimate may do you out of business with consumers who have no choice but to pay that extra VAT. Businesses that are VAT registered can claim any VAT back, where as consumers cannot. Take advice from your accountant on this.

Ultimately if you want to grow then at some point you will hit the threshold and at that point you will have no choice.

When we first registered for VAT five years ago, we claimed back some VAT on our first return, which meant the VAT department owed us money. As a result, the VAT inspector wanted to meet us to discuss the claim; he visited us at the office and scrutinised our books. A VAT inspection by a tax inspector makes everyone feel nervous but actually there was no need. The VAT inspector commented on how meticulous we had been in record keeping, and in addition, he pointed out some areas that we could claim VAT that we hadn't considered.

Having accurate bookkeeping records is just good administration.

Your bookkeeper can also deliver you accurate reports on your monthly profit and loss accounts which allows you to estimate your tax liability, so you can adequately prepare for your tax bill at the end of the financial year.

Just make sure when you do hire a bookkeeper, they understand your business, because if they don't, then they can create problems for your accountant. This can be simply rectified by setting up a meeting with your accountant and your bookkeeper so that they are in tune with which software to use, and can align the VAT quarters at the start and end of the financial and fiscal year. This can all be managed quite easily, but you need to facilitate it.

One last thing, your bookkeeper will need to create departments for your day-to-day book keeping, and this should also be discussed with your accountant. Setting up this step will allow you to track expenditure across your business.

Hire a good accountant who understands your business

I have always hired accountants to process my end of year tax reports. When you hire an accountant you're hiring someone who hopefully has an in-depth knowledge of the current taxation laws in your country and can advise you about the most efficient ways in which you can run your business. Taxation rules change on a regular basis, especially when there is a change of government. A good accountant will advise you of tax breaks, liabilities and when there are opportunities to take advantage of. Governments will often introduce different legislation that may benefit a small business owner. A good accountant will advise you on the most efficient ways to run your business finances.

An accountant may also submit annual returns for Companies House (in the UK) or equivalent depending on the country you operate in, and manage any other legal responsibilities you have as a director of a company. I cannot emphasise how important a skilled and experienced accountant is, in guiding you in running a legally compliant business and advising you on the most efficient methods of managing your tax liabilities. Spend some time speaking with trusted advisers in locating a good accountant, as this will save you time and money.

If the taxation office decides to do an audit on your business (which can be completely random) your accountant will help you navigate through that process and work on your behalf to minimise any liabilities that arise.

There's Money In Paperwork

I have learnt to be more studious and detailed in my record-keeping and business paperwork since starting the limited company. Prior to that I was employed and before that I was a freelance cameraman who was always busy and whilst I would store my receipts, I'd often spend two to three days at the end of the year wading through them to get the paperwork together for my accountant. I probably lost hundreds if not thousands of pounds worth of legitimate expense claims, because of ineffective record-keeping. Thankfully as I got older, I recognised the importance of accurate bookkeeping.

Every receipt that you can collect in relation to running your business should be submitted to your bookkeeper and accountant. These legitimate expenses are then subtracted from your gross profit at the end of the financial year and you're left with your net profit. This is then what you're taxed on, so even small amounts of parking can add up throughout the year and can legitimately reduce your tax liability.

There are a number of ways to manage your receipts and expenses. In the past, I used to sticky tape each receipt onto a piece of paper, number them and create a line item on a spreadsheet for reference. I used to hate doing this and sometimes my wife would do it for me, when she worked in the business. Thankfully, there are now other methods of doing this. I use an app called **Receipt Bank,** which has literally changed my life. I take a photograph of every receipt I get - as and when – and I upload it to receipt bank. They then take the data from the receipt (including the currency type) and input that data into a spreadsheet. My bookkeeper then has access to the app and every few days she gets an updated spreadsheet with all my recent expenses. I then archive the physical receipt back at the office, but the digital copy is stored in the cloud should it ever need to be referenced.

No matter how much you detest doing paperwork, remember - "it may be boring, but there's money in paperwork".

▣ For more resources I use, visit www.businessforfilmmakers.com/business-finances

Business banking

It is vital that you set up a separate business bank account and a business savings account that is distinct from your own personal finances. It's not uncommon to start a business and have the money come into your personal account. Certainly when I was a freelance cameraman, I began like this. However, when you begin a limited company, having a clear distinction between your personal finances and your business finances is imperative.

As your business grows, you may find yourself having multi-currency bank accounts. We have US dollar, Euro and GBP bank accounts in our business because we deal with companies across Europe and the United States, and we make it easy for clients to pay us. Sometimes this mean that we lose money on foreign exchange transactions. However, any losses are written down against tax liability. Equally, if we gain money then that is added to our gross profit. Unfortunately, we always seem to lose money when making transactions back into a base currency, and that's largely because of the banks charges, so please be aware of this and build it into your contingency.

Don't be afraid to change your bank if you're not happy. They are after all, just a supplier; it just happens to be money that they supply.

The advantage of setting up a separate business savings account is that if you charge VAT or equivalent, you can separate that money as soon as an invoice is paid. VAT in the UK is payable every quarter and is currently at 20%. This money doesn't belongs to you; you're collecting it on behalf of the government and you're liable to pay that back. Do not ever be tempted to think of that money as yours.

We have a very strict policy in our business; I separate the VAT as soon as an invoice is paid and put it into the tax and VAT savings account. I also monitor my monthly profit and loss and put a percentage away into the tax account as well, so that when my financial year is up, I know my tax liability is sitting there when it is due for payment.

It's a very risky strategy to spend the money you earn, and then when your tax bill is due you don't have enough money set aside to pay it. I strongly advise you to set aside tax and VAT money as soon as you receive it.

It's also important that you set up an overdraft facility with your bank. There may be times when you're waiting on an invoice, and more money is going out of your accounts than coming in. Having a business overdraft facility will see you through those periods and keep you afloat.

Maintaining good business records

I spend on average of one morning per week maintaining business paperwork and business admin. As a company director and principal, I personally sign all cheques and manage all banking. I strongly advise you to do the same.

I learned this from none other than Richard Branson whom I had the good fortune to meet a few years ago. I've also had other business owners share this advice with me. The reason it's so important is that you can see exactly how much money is coming and going from your business. By signing every cheque and seeing every expense that leaves your bank account, you can continually monitor your expenditure.

It is absolutely vital - especially when starting out in business - that you only spend what you absolutely need to. It's very easy to spend money on things you don't actually need, especially if, like me, you like buying gear.

Get your business off the ground, make it profitable and then there will be plenty of time to spend profits on fancy bits of gear.

Spending one morning a week managing your business keeps you grounded and in touch with how it's doing. I create invoices and at the same time input that information to the 'invoice register' - which is simply a spreadsheet – which allows me to track when invoices are due to be paid, which in turn allows me to manage cash flow.

Accurately monitoring your cash flow is the single most important thing you can do in your business. I advise maintaining an accurate cash flow spreadsheet so you know when money is coming in and money is going out.

Paperwork does not have to be complicated; you can keep it really simple. Remember, money in, money out. Just make sure that the person who is responsible for this has a vested interest in the business (one of the reasons why I do it myself). You should know at all times how much cash you have in the bank, what you are liabilities are and who owes you money. A good bookkeeper will help you with this, especially when it comes to your VAT liability.

Having good visibility across your accountancy and business admin will minimise any surprises and allow you to focus on growing your business.

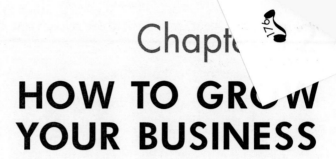

HOW TO GROW YOUR BUSINESS

The 3 Ways To Grow Your Business

There is a science and an art to business. But you should be aware that there are only three ways to grow a business.

1) **Get more customers**
2) **Increase your average order value**
3) **Sell more frequently to existing clients**

Let's look at these in turn:

Get more customers

The most obvious approach to increasing your business turnover is to sell to a larger group of customers. If you currently sell your services to 10 customers a year and generate £3,000 per customer, then your turnover will be £30,000.

If you were to increase that by 30% (to 13 customers) who spend £3,000, your turnover will increase to £39,000. Simply by adding three more customers per year, you've increased your turnover by £9,000 (30%).

Increasing average order value

If you could increase the average order by 30%, thus turning a £3000 project into £4000 a project, even at the base rate of 10 ustomers per year, you would increase your turnover from £30,000 to £40,000 per year.

Sell more frequently to those customers

Let's now imagine that 30% of your existing 10 customers bought from you a second time, then you could add approximately £9000 of additional revenue to your annual turnover. With only three customers out of those 10 buying a second £3000 project, you will increase your turnover from £30,000 to £39,000.

What makes this really cool is that if you increase each of these three areas simultaneously by 30%, you won't just increase your revenue by 30%, you'll more than double it!

Your current position

Number of existing customers = 10

Current order value - £3000 per order

Purchase frequency one x per year

Total revenue £30,000

Strategy

Increase customers by 30%

Increase average order value by 30%

Increase order frequency by 30%

Increased revenue would look like this:

30% more customers alone would yield the following:

10 customers @ £3000 = £30,000

13 customers @ £3000 = £39,000

30% increase in average order value would see an increase like this:

10 orders each @ £3000 = £30,000

10 orders each @ £4000 = £40,000

30% increase in frequency would grow your bottom line as follows:

10 customers order once @ £3000 = £30,000

3 customers order twice and spend an additional £3000 each = £39,000

The science part is where it gets really clever because if you do all three simultaneously here is what happens:

30% more customers - 13 @ £3000 = £39,000

30% increase in average order value - 13 @ £4000 = £52,000

30% increase in frequency - 30% of £52,000 = £15,600

New Annual Turnover = £67,600 against an existing T/O of £30,000

An increase of £37,600 thus doubling your business with only 30% increase across the three areas above.

Would you like to increase the amount of money your business makes by 100%?

This is exactly the formula you need to apply in order to do so. Simple.

Increase Your Prices...It's Vital To Grow

Increasing prices is such an important part of growing your business that I want to discuss it in more detail. It's all about refinement and repositioning you and your business away from a cheap product to a desirable and premium priced service.

Low cost, high quality and speed cannot coexist, and the kind of clients you want to be dealing with are people who understand this.

Speed

Take something as simple as ordering a product from an online retailer. If the item is in stock then you can usually select a variety of shipping methods, all priced accordingly. If you want that item the next day before 9am, then the shipping option for this is likely to be the most expensive compared to the standard shipping, which takes two to three days. What this demonstrates is that if you want the item quickly, you pay a premium price. If you don't need it right away, then you choose a more economical shipping option. Speed and efficiency is more expensive than slow and economical.

If you apply the same principles to your video productions, you can charge a premium for post-production if the client wants the item delivered quickly. There's no reason why you can't charge a 50% additional premium on your edit rates for a quick turnaround.

Quality

Let's imagine your client would like a very high production promotional film that they want to have a cinematic look and feel to. This will require you to work with the gaffer and additional lighting, perhaps a focus puller, a grip, and other production team that might include actors, make-up people, and a costume department. Your DP might choose a camera format like the Red Epic, Arri Alexa, or a Sony F55 with cine lenses and associated camera package. It's also likely it would take one or two days to shoot in a single location, taking care with every single frame. However, if the client wanted this kind of high quality production, but only wanted a three hour shoot, then there would be a disconnect from the amount of time required to the quality of the end production. If they want quality, it takes time and money.

High quality is generally associated with the addition of the best resources to guarantee the consistency of output.

Low cost

You never want to be associated with cheap. There are plenty of videographers out there working with cheap equipment and the bare minimum of gear, fighting over who can do the job the cheapest. You never want to be in a race to the bottom. If you find yourself in a position where you're being price matched with another company, then the chances are you're dealing with the wrong kinds of clients. You probably haven't got a strong enough relationship with that client either.

Priced-based buyers are not interested in relationships, they are only interested in getting the cheapest price and that is not a business I recommend you focus on.

If you are too cheap your clients will not take you seriously and it gives out the wrong message. Increasing your prices to a point where you're reassuringly expensive gives you the pleasure of dealing with non priced based buyers.

Be reassuringly expensive

Raising your prices will feel uncomfortable; in fact, when you deliver your costs to a client, if you don't feel a little uncomfortable, then the chances are you're not charging enough.

Also, never give your prices verbally. The danger of giving pricing this way is when you announce your price, the line goes silent and you lose your bottle and risk saying something daft like, *"but if it's too much, I can do you a deal"*. Be proud of your prices; if you're pricing correctly you can dedicate your time to the client project and give them a premium service.

A good friend of mine runs a very successful coaching and consulting business and he works with CEOs and senior managers across blue-chip companies. A couple of years ago he bought himself a Bentley Continental, with cash. I think the car cost in excess of £150,000. For many people, that kind of money is out of the realms of possibility. However, even if you have the money, when you buy that car from Bentley you have to wait. Premium brands often employ scarcity in their sales process as it helps to further enhance the exclusivity of ownership. Plus, when you do order the car it is hand built to your specification and the person who builds it inscribes their name within the chassis. Then each year, when the car needs a service, the engineer who built the car comes personally to the home of the owner and services the car.

Bentley is a premium brand, and my friend is happy to pay the higher prices to have the person who built the car come and service his car. He has the means to pay for such a car and such a service. He doesn't have to wait in line at a garage, it's all done for him which allows him to focus on making money in his own business.

He also travels everywhere in either business or first class, and only ever invests in the best products and services because he likes the fact that buying from premium priced brands delivers him a premium service.

Don't *ever underestimate* the value clients put on dealing with a company that is focused on high quality and service. Many are willing to pay more than you think for video production.

You may not feel your business is currently in that position. That's okay, reading this book and applying the principles I share with you will begin to move you more decisively in that direction.

As a side note, when I decided to write this book I knew I had to clear my diary for around six weeks so I could focus on writing. I've built my business so I don't have to generate any new business for six weeks and I have enough resources to enable me to take time out and focus on this project. I can do that because I charge premium rates for my time. I'm also doing a couple of events next month and the money generated from two days of work exceeds what I used to earn after tax, in a month, five years ago. That's the equivalent of a 10 x increase in my earning potential in only five years. I put this down specifically to investing in business education, coaches and consultants because they have encouraged me to continually increase my prices and position myself as a premium brand.

None of this happened without focused implementation.

As a cameraman I used to go out for anywhere between £200 and £350 per day. Today, my starting point is £1500 per day. Interestingly, when pricing yourself higher, you start to attract clients who are much easier to work with.

I also make sure that I don't rely on any one client for a significant portion of my annual business. Premium pricing and diversifying my business has allowed me to be in this position. No one client (if they stop working with me) would have a detrimental affect on my overall livelihood. This means I am in a very strong bargaining position when discussing client projects because I am willing to walk away if the terms and project don't suit me.

When you charge premium prices and your revenues begin to grow, you have many more choices. However, one word of warning... *leave your ego in a box in the office.* When clients are paying premium prices, they do not want to deal with precious creative egos.

Immunity to criticism

You have to make a plan for business growth, both strategic and personal. I largely ignore what most of my *'peers'* are doing online or otherwise. In my mind, I don't have any competition. We offer something unique and our clients value our contribution.

When you begin to become more successful, you will attract criticism. Any competitors in your marketplace will see what you're doing and will try to discredit you. This is a good sign that you're doing things right.

Markets and industries like to keep things on an even keel. I mentioned in a previous chapter about how *'industry standard'* simply means the lowest common denominator that the industry and clients in that marketplace are willing to accept. When someone comes along and disrupts the status quo, it causes waves.

Blackmagic Design have done just that in the camera sector by creating very affordable cinema quality cameras. All the major camera manufacturers have since responded with lower cost, higher feature based competing products. I'm almost certain that had Blackmagic not come out with the Blackmagic Cinema Camera, the other major camera manufacturers would not be responding as quickly or at price points that are so affordable.

When Blackmagic were having trouble fulfilling orders with the first batch of cinema cameras, they got a lot of stick within the social media space. But talk is cheap and individuals hide behind social media and laptops, criticising from afar. It's very easy to point the finger and throw blame at individuals and organisations.

You have to learn to ignore any criticism and negativity aimed at you and your business. Remember, social media is elective. If someone starts throwing abuse at you or indirectly trying to undermine you, simply unfollow and block. My advice is to eliminate any negative influences that creep into your business.

People can be very jealous when you begin to succeed. They don't understand, and some respond by either ignoring you publicly or making indirect remarks within the circle you operate in. Social media specifically can be very cliquey, and often the people who are on there the most, are the ones working the least.

Learn to grow a thick skin and ignore any criticism pointed at you and your company. A business is not a democracy, it is your business that you set up, risking everything for and working more hours than your colleagues and friends.

You may find friends you've known for a long time become a little hostile towards you when you start to see success. The trouble is, they don't see you working 16-18 hours a day in the beginning to get your business off the ground. They don't have a clue what it's like to not have a consistent income coming in every month. They don't experience waking up in a cold sweat at 5am panicking about how you will pay the bills next month.

Once you've implemented all the strategies and built up your client base you will reach a plateau which I call the *'tipping point'* of your business when things just start to snowball. It took me four years to reach a point where the business could become predictable. You must never give up, and if you believe you have a business that helps clients and that you can charge a premium rate for, you will succeed.

Never give up because success can be just around the next corner. Just look at the number of music artists who seem to come from nowhere and appear to be an overnight success! You just haven't seen the five years of playing pubs and clubs before they got a record deal.

Enjoy your successes along the way

When you begin to make money, enjoy it.

In the few cases I've experienced any negativity is simply down to jealousy. The harsh reality for friends or family who have trouble accepting your new success is that it just goes to compound their own lack of success. When you decide to put a stake in the ground and build a business that will create freedom for you and your family, it can leave some people behind.

However, there are so many benefits to running your own business, especially if you're able get involved in mastermind groups of other business owners and entrepreneurs who share the same passion. I have a number of mentors, and they are all far more successful in business than I am. I love that fact, because I have so much still to learn. Only ever take advice from people who are more successful than you and just ignore anyone who throws criticism in your direction.

I occasionally have people who want to offer me feedback on how they believe I should be running my company. If you've been on my email list for a while, then you will see me talk about this when people try to offer me their 'feedback'.

We live in a culture that seems to promote the notion that the customer is always right and that even potential customers are free to give you their opinion and feedback on how you should run your business. Number one: I only ever listen to customers who are paying me currently. Number two: unless you're paying me, I have very little interest in your opinion.

Not All Customers Are Created Equal

At the time of writing this book, our lowest cost product at www.fstopacademy.com sells for US $49 and the most expensive programme sells for US $897. The customer who spends $49 does not get treated the same way as a customer who spends $897. That is because the customer who spends $897 is spending 18 times more than the customer spending $49.

Treat your highest paying clients and customers differently to your lower paying clients and customers.

Interestingly, the higher paying customers - who are paying 18 times more are usually far more pleasant to deal with. Now, I'm not suggesting that all customers paying $49 are not enjoyable to deal with, but in some cases when customers spend less they can suck a lot of your time, for not much reward.

Selling a product for $897 to one person, as opposed to dealing with 18 customers at $49, helps you to begin to understand where I'm coming from.

Incidentally, the $49 products are mostly legacy products and we'll be phasing them out in due course in favour of more consolidated programs.

In another example, when we run our in-person workshops, we minimise the class size to between six and eight people. A two-day lighting class costs £895, but you're guaranteed to be in a class size of no more than eight, which means you get one on one time from me and ample time asking all the questions you may have about how to improve your lighting. These classes are very interactive and very practical, and every attendee walks away having lit at least one setup while actively participating in another seven. The net result is that after two days you walk away from the class with confidence and the knowledge to light an interview in any situation.

Our classes always sell out. We always have great candidates and after the class they become a member of a private Facebook group where they can continue to share and learn from each other.

We often get emails from filmmakers saying they can't afford to join the class, and could we offer the class at £150 per person for two days. If we offered the class for £150 per person, we would have to sell 47 places to generate the same revenue as the higher priced service. If we chose to do that the experience would be totally different and there would be no hands-on training. There would also be far more administration involved in registering 47 attendees, following up and ensuring they had all the information required to attend the class.

I have always had the policy of focusing on smaller numbers of the right kind of customers. This means positioning myself as a premium educator, which in turn attracts a higher quality customer, all of whom I would happily go out for a beer with. I have engineers, surgeons, airline pilots, IT professionals, CEOs, senior management and entrepreneurs who value coming to spend time in a class with me to learn about hands-on practical filmmaking technique. Many have come back repeatedly to do different courses with us.

You do not need to have hundreds of people giving you money to run a successful business. Focus on your niche and specialise in attracting businesses who have the resources to invest in high-quality video.

Specialise and become the market leader

Niching what you do is critical to your overall success. If you want to specialise in two or three different niches then treat them as separate entities under the same umbrella.

If you specialise in shooting high-quality customer testimonial videos for clients then that could be the primary function of your business. That client may call upon you to create other video content as a result. Clients like to have a set of suppliers they know they can rely on. The more value you bring to a client, the more likely they are to ask you to do more work.

If you specialise in creating customer testimonial videos, then become the leading supplier of customer testimonial video production in your area. When you position yourself as the outstanding expert in your field, things happen. Your competition will start to panic and clients will probably want to work with the market leader and not the jack-of-all-trades video producer.

Why not create a PDF guide to help clients who are looking to create customer testimonial videos, and help guide them in the process. We talked about this strategy earlier in creating 'free line' content to attract prospects in return for their email addresses. If you want to go further, then you could write a book on the subject. Writing a book is not as difficult as it might seem. You have to plan it, break it down and then get on and write it.

You could write a small book of maybe 60 to 100 pages. Writing a book automatically positions you as an expert. If you are a video production business specialising in a particular niche and you have written a book about the considerations clients should think about when searching for a supplier, then you automatically become an expert in that field. You will automatically stand out from the general video production businesses. I've mentioned this before, but I'm writing this book primarily to position myself as the world's leading authority on business for filmmakers.

To my knowledge, there is not another book on the planet that covers this topic in this level of detail. I am therefore, by default, *'the world's leading authority on business for filmmakers'*. It's self-proclaimed, but nobody will challenge me (and if they do, they'd need to be the author of a book on the subject to even stand a chance of me taking them seriously).

A friend of mine, Kat, runs a high quality hairdressing salon in London's Notting Hill. Her business is growing exponentially as a result of positioning, and providing a great service at a premium price. Guess what they've also done? Terry, who is Kat's business partner, has just written a book. The book is called *'101 Naked Confessions of a Gay Hairdresser – the secrets to fabulous hair from the world's most outrageous hairdresser'*. How many hairdressers do you know have written a book? Already the salon has a list of pre-orders. This is premium positioning in action, and the willingness of Kat and Terry to put together a book will only add more gravitas to their business. After all, if you consider two salons within a mile of each other and one guy has written a book on achieving wonderful hair and the other hasn't, the very fact that the competitor has not, starts to devalue their service.

Anything you do in marketing that positions you ahead of your competition immediately makes them look like they can't compete with your service.

Work hard, stay focused, be confident

There are certain processes that you have to go through when building a business; they take time and there are not really any shortcuts. But there are things you can do that are more profitable than others and it's these that you should priortise.

There are high value tasks you can be performing in your business, and low value ones. When you begin a business it is likely you will be doing most of the work yourself, but as you grow it's worth getting help from other people to take off some of the pressure.

Running a business can be stressful, exhausting and frustrating at times. However, it can also be the most *liberating, enjoyable* and *the greatest personal confidence building exercise you will ever likely achieve.* Building a business that creates freedom for you and your family means that in the future, you can choose how much you work and never having to ask the boss to take time off to go on vacation.

Clients like dealing with confident suppliers. It helps them relax.

You don't have to build your business alone. While the ultimate responsibility for the success or failure of your business will rest on your shoulders, there are many resources available to help you succeed.

The good news is, you're not the first person to begin a start-up business or try to grow an existing one. There are plenty of resources available in the marketplace to help businesses in all sorts of capacities. Choose the ones that are most likely to suit where you want to go in business, and only choose people who have already done it before you.

Modelling yourself on other successful people is a great way of growing in confidence and skills. But be careful, because trying to reverse engineer someone else's business model can be dangerous if you don't fully understand the motivation behind a certain approach.

Chapter 13
HOW TO 'MAKE IT' FASTER

How Exactly Do You Do It?

I wanted to write this book because the journey from conceiving a business idea and migrating, as I did, from freelance to employee to business owner, was a huge learning curve. It has been one of the most exciting challenges I've ever taken on in my life. It's also been responsible for some of the most stressful and anxiety filled days I've experienced. At times it can seem like an impossibly huge task. The learning curve is steep; *growing a business is possibly one of the hardest things you will ever do.*

But for me, the decision to take it on was easy because the alternative of maintaining a position as an employee was not something I was willing to settle for.

Make no mistake, if you embrace entrepreneurism and dedicate everything you have to making your business a success, the rewards go way beyond financial. For me, it's always been about *freedom.*

One of the key driving factors for me establishing my own business was simply down to the fact that in my last staff job I was only entitled to 20 days vacation per year. I also had to ask permission from my boss to take it. I hated that. So I did something about it.

I also wanted to earn more money. There were certain things I wanted to buy that I couldn't afford on my existing salary. There were vacations I wanted to go on, I wanted to travel business class not economy when flying, and I wanted to stay in five star hotels when I took my wife and family on vacation.

I have a number of friends who have a net worth in excess of £1 million. Net worth is when they actually can access £1 million in cash at a moment's notice. And while I'm not specifically driven by money per se, I do enjoy the freedom it brings and the choices it gives you.

The most important thing I've discovered about running my own business is that I decide how much money to earn, it gives me good cash flow and it allows me to be picky with who I work with.

We can go on vacation whenever I like, (my wife also runs her own business). And now my step-sons, Oliver and Barney are older, we can take off pretty much on a whim if we choose to. That's freedom for me.

My goal is to continue nurturing and growing a business that can deliver me a consistent income as well as helping other people to achieve their goals. This allows me to balance my own entrepreneurial desires, as well as giving me the freedom to spend quality time with my friends and family.

I am 43 years old and love my life. I have a wonderful business which keeps growing, wonderful customers - many of them I regard as friends – and my wife and I have a great relationship. We have some exciting plans that will transform our lifestyle in the coming 12 months.

I have learnt so much since starting the company and the most important and significant lesson that I can share with you is to *never underestimate* what you can do as an individual. I realised that I had a number of limiting beliefs before I started this business, but anything is possible with a solid plan and adequate resources.

Running a successful business does not have to be a mystery, there are so many business resources available to you, and they explain exactly how to do it. In order to succeed you need to follow a set number of steps, and whether those steps take five years or 12 months is simply down to what you can put in place to achieve it. With unlimited financial resources you can achieve the steps faster but for many, organic growth takes a little more time.

If you've got to the stage in the book and are now thinking *"can I do it?"* the answer is yes! But don't underestimate the scale of the task ahead. Getting help will allow you to do it faster.

Getting Help

Be very careful who you take business advice from.

When you announce that you going to start a business, be prepared for a varying mix of responses. Some people close to you may express fear and reservations at the risks involved. Try not to take too much of that on board. Human nature means that when you step out of the norm and go in a different direction from the masses (and mass consensus is to stay safe and play by the rules) people will express their own fears and try to put them on you.

Entrepreneurs ignore the rules.

I was very fortunate to meet a guy early on when we started the business who was very successful in his own business and had recently sold it for a significant sum of money. He offered me incredible advice right from the start and has become a very close friend in the last five years.

Interestingly, as my business career has matured, so has my circle of friends. Most of whom are highly successful, highly motivated business owners. Associating with other successful people has a very positive impact on your mindset and ultimately your business.

Discovering new strategies and studying other successful people is the most enriching aspect of being an entrepreneur. There are some wonderful books on this subject and if you take only one or two ideas from each book and implement them in your own business, you will see dramatic results.

I cannot emphasise enough how important continual education is as a business owner.

I have spent in excess of £50,000 over the last five years on business education, working with coaches and taking part in business mastermind groups.

Every time I invest in *myself, my business grows.* In year three we worked with a business coach and during that 12 month period I established higher day rates, which had a dramatic impact on how I perceive myself and how my clients perceive me. We also made more money by implementing that, so the cost of that training was effectively free.

Even if you don't yet run a business, investing in education, seminars and online programs will help prepare you for the day you decide to go it alone. Do not risk starting a business without some professional help. There are mistakes you will make from day one that could cost you dearly and ultimately cost you your business.

I spent thousands on business education and studied sales and marketing for three years prior to starting my business. I used my salary and spent my evenings and weekends studying, so that I could best prepare myself for when I took the decision to start my own business. It's not that hard, just turn off the TV and invest in your future.

Joining a mastermind group

When your business reaches a point where you're doing okay but are struggling to get beyond a certain level of turnover, then I strongly advise seeking out either a coach or, even better still, joining a mastermind group. A mastermind group is where a small group of business owners get together two or three times per year to set goals and be accountable for them. These groups often meet in locations away from your actual business, which forces you to spend two days focusing *'on your business'* and where you want to go, and not focusing on working *'in your business'*.

If you are intereseted in learning more about my Elite coaching group and feel that you are ready to take the next step, you can learn about the application criteria at www.businessforfilmmakers.com/elite-mastermind

The value of being in such a coaching group is almost immeasurable because listening to other business owners talk about problems and challenges they face helps you understand that you're not alone. Business is business, people are people and whether or not you sell widgets, are in manufacturing, or run a video production business, the principles of selling to people are the same.

However, there is one caveat; your business has to be ready and financially stable before you invest in a high-end coaching group. But if you want to take your business to six figures and beyond, then joining a coaching group will accelerate that process.

I speak from personal experience because I am a member of an elite coaching group, in addition to running one myself. In fact, the reason this book exists is a direct result of being a member of that coaching group. In the last 12 months eight of the 14 have written books positioning their expertise.

Everyone who is a member of the coaching group has seen the business increase by at least 30 to 50% and in some cases far more.

The key success driver is *accountability*. We're also a pretty competitive bunch and we're always trying to outdo each other, and that's very healthy for business growth.

Having a group of people who share your passion for business means you have people you can call, discuss challenges with and share your successes. It's one of the best investments you can make, and the experience has effectively cost me nothing because I've made so much more money as a result of being part of that group. I wouldn't have managed that had I been trying to do it alone.

Being a part of the coaching group forces you to be accountable and to implement ideas and strategies that will grow your business.

Implementation

There is work involved in growing a business; it's one thing to study and digest the information in this book, but you actually have to *do it* and **apply it** to your business for it to be a success. Implementing strategies and testing marketing campaigns takes time and much of it may not work. Being a great marketer and entrepreneur is in the understanding that as much as 90% of what you do may fail. But every failure is a lesson in understanding what doesn't work in your business and will take you one step closer to identifying what does. Once you identify what that is, you simply do more of it. Most people give up too easily and it's hard when it feels like you're crawling up a hill in soft sand.

You have to be very disciplined and very honest with yourself if you want to succeed. Running a business is not for everyone. You have to have an inner core of strength and believe that you will succeed, and you need the tenacity to keep going until you do. It is risky, which is why so many businesses fail in the first 12 months and 80% fail within the first five years. You need to be sure that you can generate significant revenue to pay all your taxes, fulfil all your legal obligations and have some money left to live on.

Business can be a cruel mistress, but by applying the principles I have shared with you in this book and implementing the strategies, you will discover what will work.

It's definitely not easy but it is very straightforward, it just takes focus and determination. You will have to make some pretty significant sacrifices in the early years, but take it from me when it starts to work the rewards come thick and fast. You simply need to have the right mindset, be motivated and implement everything you learn.

As I near the end of this book, I cannot tell you the sense of pride I have in the fact I've just written in excess of 60,000 words on this topic. I never would have believed it possible. It helps that I'm pretty stubborn, and you'll discover that stubbornness and an unwillingness to accept failure as a reason to stop is a common trait in successful business owners and entrepreneurs.

Do not underestimate what you're capable of and never give up.

If you serve your customers well - the money will come

The recipe for success is relatively simple: solve the problems your customers face, serve them well, and the money will come. Don't focus solely on the money; focus on solving problems and helping customers communicate their message through great looking video. *Price yourself accordingly, and your business will profit.*

Focus on providing value and become a trusted supplier that your customers just *'can't do without'*. Clients want an easy life and a great result from their investment. In many cases, if you're dealing with a marketing manager, their measure of success is twofold. Did the project meet its objectives? I.e. successful market penetration, number of views, number of sales - or all of the above. Did they enjoy working with you and did they get a good return on their investment? Did the senior stakeholders in the company approve and see value from the investment? Did you make that marketing manager look good in front of their boss? Because as I said before, people buy from people and everyone's accountable to someone else.

Never Stop Learning

The best investment you can make for your business is in yourself. It's very easy to focus on investing in equipment - I know because I've been there - but nothing is more debilitating than having a bunch of gear sitting on a shelf not earning you money.

I recently sold a big load of gear I had because I'm now more involved with business coaching, and in doing so I created a lightness in my own mind.

The productions we work on now, I work as a producer and we hire in equipment specifically for that job. Businesses are always changing and I no longer need to own a high-end shooting package. My main camera now is a Sony Alpha 7S and I also have a couple of Blackmagic Cinema Cameras. That's more than enough for me to shoot the educational videos I record here in the studio.

I now spend more of my time studying, reading and learning about sales, marketing, the psychology of selling, and how to grow a successful business. I invest in these so I can digest the information and share it with my own filmmaking coaching groups.

▢   If you don't feel ready or qualified to join one of our Elite Coaching Programs, but want to learn more about how you can work with me personally, follow this link to www.businessforfilmmakers.com/inner-circle

We offer a number of different programs to help you achieve your filmmaking business goals.

You may be starting out or you may already be established, either way we have resources that will help you to succeed and achieve your goals.

Financial freedom is a choice and you can make a very good living running a boutique video production business that satisfies your creativity and generates a six-figure plus income for you and your family. There has never been a better time to offer video production services to the business marketplace. Video is everywhere; we are consuming more video now than ever. So there are many opportunities available for you.

Be true to your vision

As we come to the final part of the book, I have one more bit of advice. *Stay focused on your vision, work hard, be diligent and enjoy it.* But use 80/20 thinking. Working hard on the wrong things is not congruent with working smart.

I advocate doing everything in your own business at the very beginning, so you at least understand intimately what each process in your business consists of, and the resources that are required to carry it out effectively.

It may be that you shoot and edit everything yourself in the early days, partly because it makes sense and partly because you make more money. But at some point you will no longer be able to do all of those roles effectively.

When you start to grow, outsourcing production elements to a good solid crew and working with great editors and other talented people will result in you having even better products for your customers, allowing you to focus on being a producer and running your business.

The key to success is moving away from being a help for hire and offering the 'full service production facility', involving the creative and practical delivery of the products.

Building a sustainable business and a solid client base will give you the lifestyle and financial resources you desire. Never underestimate what you're personally capable of, and enjoy the experience. There is nothing more rewarding than helping customers grow.

On a recent project we completed for Sony, the senior management were so impressed with the final film that they arranged to show it to the CEO. That in itself was a great accolade, but more rewarding was seeing the faces of the management who had employed us as they discussed it with each other. This was a huge deal for them and gave specific visibility to their department in front of the most senior member of management. That made them extremely proud of their achievement and they thanked me for it personally.

While that does not guarantee work in the future, it certainly goes down as a positive tick in the box. When a new project arises it will be a clean slate and that is the way that business should run, because you should never take it for granted and get comfortable.

... Oh Yes, And Lastly... Be Yourself!

Be you, speak and write in your own voice and be proud of who you are. Nothing says integrity more than being consistent with your communications. I write all my emails myself. I don't give off some pseudo bullshit public relations persona. I am me, and if I'm honest, I'm a bit like Marmite; you either love me or you hate me, and I'm okay with both. Because the only people I'm interested in really is my customers. Everyone else's opinion is irrelevant.

Nothing is more rewarding than working hard to build a business, then watching it grow and succeed.

I am also most proud of the filmmakers who have trusted me to help them achieve greater success. When I read the emails from customers telling me how they've applied lessons they've learned from me and are now enjoying greater success as a result, I feel incredibly proud because they have implemented advice I've given, and are now more successful and enjoy greater happiness as a result.

Life is relatively short, so make sure you are living life to the full and that you are building a future for you and your family that can provide you freedom – and don't forget to enjoy it along the way!

Wishing you every success, now what are you waiting for?

Conclusion

So what's next for you? I've shared dozens of strategies and approaches that if you implement just a few of them, will transform your business, guaranteed! But it's one thing to read and nod in agreement, quite another to actually *do it*.

But that's OK, you are not alone. I started where you are. If you diligently apply yourself and follow the strategies I have shared with you, then step-by-step and day-by-day you *will* move measurably closer to your desired goals.

This is the beginning of a very exciting and rewarding journey for you, but be under no illusion, it is not always going to be an easy road.

The process is unbelievably simple, yes, but it does involve effort to get it going. Since setting up www.fstopacademy.com in 2009, I have continually been amazed at how much work is involved in keeping things simple. You will discover this for yourself.

If you take only one tactic from this book, then create a free report for your target market that offers true genuine value in exchange for an email address. Then set up a series of emails using an email auto responder that then serve to build a relationship with your target audience. This alone will transform how prospects and customers view you and your business. When you break the back of it, you will have a systemised process in place for attracting only your ideal customer. And that is an awesome feeling.

Remember: *marketing is everything and everything is marketing.*

Much of what I've shared in this book may be alien to you or even make you feel a little uncomfortable, but don't give up because stepping outside your comfort zone will advance you further than you ever thought possible. That I *promise* you.

I was sent a link recently on Facebook and it sums up in a nutshell how I feel about life now.

"When you truly don't care what the fuck people think of you, you have reached a dangerously AWESOME LEVEL of FREEDOM."

I rather like it...

Den

About The Author

My story is unusual. When I was at school I was picked on, and so I found solace in being the school videographer. We had a VHS camcorder that sat in a cupboard on the second floor and we had an audio visual guy who came into the school once a fortnight. So at 14 years old, I made it my goal to befriend him so that I could get my hands on the camcorder. It was a separate camera and recorder back in those days, but nonetheless I wanted to use it to film a school play.

My other escape from the bullying was the school theatre. There was no one taking care of the lighting, so I befriended the drama teacher and asked if I could learn how to run the lighting desk.

I guess looking back, I realised the value of forming relationships with the right people early on. I cannot tell you how I knew to do this, but perhaps the isolation from being bullied taught me to stand strong on my own feet. I had a kind of 'fuck you all' attitude towards the bullies and the people around who were too scared to say anything to defend me, most probably because they figured silence meant it would not be them who got the shit.

Don't get me wrong, it was tough... name calling at school can be very hurtful and damaging to kids growing up. But after the early years in primary school, I had toughened up by high school.

I turned the negative into a positive, which has served me well ever since. Truth is, it doesn't ever go away. People still bully online, not me, I have to say - I am well beyond letting any fucktard online call me names, criticise or indeed offer their opinion on how I should run my life or business, and if you are on my email list then you will have seen how I deal with idiots and criticism.

The moral of this story is that in the face of adversity you can thrive. The reason I became so passionate about lighting and shooting was initially out of a desperate need to get away from the horrible bullying. It worked.

So when the time came to go on 'work experience' at the age of 16, I rejected all of the suggested jobs of working in a music shop, factory, insurance company, and started ringing round the local radio and TV stations.

Edinburgh, where I grew up, had one local radio station, Radio Forth, and BBC Scotland had a satellite office. The main BBC office was in Glasgow 30 miles away. But I figured if I wanted to spend a week in a recording or TV studio, I was prepared to travel if needs be.

So I wrote a list (from the phonebook - this was long before Google existed), and started cold calling. I rang eight different companies and even a few production companies.... All said no.

Except the last call at 4.30pm on a Friday afternoon.

I called BBC Scotland in Edinburgh and as soon as the receptionist picked up I went off into a sales pitch about how much I wanted to learn about audio recording and TV. The power of naivety meant I had no real concept of protocol, and it worked because she put me straight through to the head of BBC Scotland in Edinburgh.

After a short call, and another sales pitch, he said yes!

I had to then get an official letter from my deputy head, but in a nutshell I'd secured a week of work experience off the back of a phone call.

I'd say this was my first major achievement and looking back my tenacity and resolve to make it happen started young. I went into the situation with a vision that someone had to say yes, and I would not stop until they did. Never give up because a yes might just be on that next call.

I then went on to spend the next seven years going back and forwards to BBC Scotland and getting to know everyone. I spent a large amount of time with a cameraman called Jim Galbreath, and a Sound recordist called Ian Cowie. They were my first true mentors and I owe them a great deal of gratitude, because they put up with me tailing them on every summer holiday and break I had from school, college and film school.

I learned a great deal from them, and I remain friends with them today.

As for the rest of my career, I got my first job with Reuters Television, as a trainee sound recordist on £9,000 per year (around $15,000) and started working on a network breakfast TV show called GMTV. After two and half years learning to record sound, edit and begin shooting, I applied for a job with the BBC and got it. This was a post in East Anglia and I lasted 11 months before another opportunity came up to work on London's flagship independent news programme, 'London Today/London Tonight'. This was brilliant, more money, a company car and a four day working week and a lot of variety. I'd gone from regional news in East Anglia to shooting Tom Cruise, Kylie, and a host of other celebrity news.

After three years shooting a wide variety of genres and playing my part in a Royal Television Society Award for our coverage of the Soho Nail Bomb, I went freelance. (Technically, I can call myself an award winning cameraman... but it seems that if you win a prize at your school play these days you can call yourself award winning. Part of the problem with self publicity and social media is that every filmmaker out there seems to be *award winning* which somewhat dilutes the value so I tend to stay away from that stuff.)

Making the leap

Speaking to other freelancers in my circle, it seems to be common that we spend around 18 months thinking (pontificating) about it and talking about it. Then one day you get a job and it's time to cut the umbilical cord from the security and regular pay a staff job offers.

For me, it was about achieving more freedom, and I wanted to shoot more interesting projects that working for a news company no longer offered.

Being a freelance technician

January 2001 was the date when I went out on my own as a freelance lighting cameraman. So I suppose that's when I truly started my first business.

In the subsequent years I travelled to over 50 countries, shooting for a host of major production companies and broadcasters all over the world. Then in 2001 I broke my ankle on a shoot in Chamonix. We were shooting a documentary following two guys who were going to parasend off the summit of Mont Blanc. Unfortunately for me I slipped on a glacier on the first day of filming - the worst fear of a freelance cameraman, 10 months into his freelance career - six months off work... bugger.

Anyway, I had insurance to cover loss of income and so I kept my apartment. If you are reading this as a freelance of any description (and don't have any insurance for this), then stop now and go and get yourself some income protection insurance that is specific to your occupation. It's alarming how many freelancers I know who do not put value on protecting themselves against injury.

My leg recovered and I went on to have a very busy 18 months until I was filming in Capetown in March 2003 and my ankle felt weird. When I got home I saw a specialist who informed me that my ankle had developed irreversible arthritis and that my career was over... just like that.

Boom....

And of course, I'd just bought a new house....

Thankfully my insurance still covered me but I racked up in excess of £30k of debt during the next six months...

I sold the house and got a job with Procam Televison (which I used to rent my gear from) as the warehouse and kit room manager. With my experience on the road, I was able to develop systems and within no time I was bringing in new business. I had a rapport and synergy with the freelance cameramen and production managers too because I knew exactly what it was like to be on a shoot and have gear not work. We quickly positioned ourselves as the market leader.

Now the technical stuff about Den

Den Lennie is a producer, DP and entrepreneur, a sought after marketing consultant, strategic advisor, author and trainer to small and medium sized video production companies.

With a 20 year track record in broadcasting and independent video production, he set up his own coaching business, and since 2009 he has helped thousands of aspiring filmmakers to grow in confidence and build successful boutique video production businesses around the world.

He is known for his no-nonsense approach.

When he is not running the international online film academy at www.fstopacademy.com, he produces a select number of high end corporate and industrial films for clients including, Sony, OConnor, Vitec Group, Tiffen, Zeiss and other leading broadcasting and video production equipment manufacturers.

He is a keen sailor and splits his time between the UK and Australia.

His UK office is in London, and his Australian office is in Sydney. Should you wish to contact him directly about speaking, consulting, or just your comments about this book you are welcome to do so by emailing office@fstopacademy.com

Ready to accelerate your video business?

Join Den's Business for Filmmakers Inner Circle

A monthly success program where you interact directly with Den and grow your video business faster with his support. Discover the benefits and how to join at: www.businessforfilmmakers.com/inner-circle/

Elite Mastermind - If you qualify and are ready for 1-2-1 support and are willing to break six figures and beyond in the next 12 months? Apply to join one of Den's Elite Coaching Groups:

www.businessforfilmmakers.com/elite-mastermind/

Other training resources by Den.

Lighting for Digital Filmmakers
www.fstopacademy.com/video-lighting-for-beginners/

How to Shoot Interviews
www.fstopacademy.com/how-to-shoot-interviews/

Advanced Video Lighting
www.fstopacademy.com/advanced-video-lighting/

How to Shoot sequences
www.fstopacademy.com/how-to-shoot-sequences/

Canon 5D Mk III Training
http://www.fstopacademy.com/canon-5d-mark-iii-video-training/

Blackmagic Camera Training
http://www.fstopacademy.com/black-magic-camera-training/